THE
SHEPHERD

ALSO BY JOSEPH F. GIRZONE:

Joshua

Joshua and the Children

Kara the Lonely Falcon

Gloria: A Diary

*Who Will Teach Me:
A Handbook for Parents*

THE SHEPHERD

JOSEPH F. GIRZONE

M&S

Copyright © 1990 by Joseph F. Girzone

Macmillan Publishing Company
866 Third Avenue, New York, NY 10022

Collier Macmillan Canada, Inc.
1200 Eglinton Avenue East, Suite 200
Don Mills, Ontario M3C 3N1

Published in Canada 1990 by McClelland & Stewart Inc.
The Canadian Publishers
481 University Avenue
Toronto, Ontario
M5G 2E9

Canadian Cataloguing in Publication Data

Girzone, Joseph F.
    The shepherd
ISBN 0-7710-3317-6
I. Title.
PS3557.I77S44 1990   813'.54   C90-095038-2

Printed in the United States of America

McClelland & Stewart Inc.
The Canadian Publishers
481 University Avenue
Toronto, Ontario M5G 2E9

THE
SHEPHERD

1

THE record-breaking winter had frozen everyone's spirits. A happy event was needed to melt the gloom and free everyone from the depression that hung over the community. The consecration as bishop of a priest who was loved by almost everyone was that event. The previous weeks, and months, had been cold and dismal, but this day seemed to make up for it all. The weather was perfect. The sun bright and warm, the crisp air fresh from the morning dew, the cool, blue sky with hardly a cloud, all hinted of an early summer. Happy voices filled the air. The sidewalks surrounding the massive Gothic cathedral were teeming with people of every race and religion. An unusual number of Jews, some with beards and long black coats, mingled with their friends; at a distance from them in another section of the crowd was a small group of Muslims, a handful wearing fezzes. There was a sprinkling of Oriental people, too. It was hard to imagine all of these people fitting into the building even as vast as it was, but its huge, bronze-framed doorways swallowed them all as they poured through.

Tommy Burns was a squat, thickly built Irishman. He and his wife, Emily, were walking toward the cathedral next to a rabbi. Tommy was curious as to why a rabbi, especially the old-fashioned kind, was going to a Catholic bishop's consecration. Never reserved, Tommy asked him.

"Rabbi, if I am not being ignorant or too forward, why would a man like yourself be coming to a bishop's consecration?" Tommy asked bluntly.

The rabbi, taken aback, answered simply, "Because he is much more than a bishop to me. Our congregation will always be indebted to David Campbell. When the state was going to take away our synagogue to build a highway, David used his influence with the governor's office to have the course of the highway moved. He is like one of our family. He visits and prays with us on many Friday nights. It is as if one of our own was being made bishop. Perhaps you could tell me why you have come to his consecration."

Tommy grinned. "About six months ago I lost my job and couldn't keep up the mortgage payments on my house. The bank was starting foreclosure proceedings. My wife and I were beside ourselves. If we couldn't afford the mortgage we wouldn't be able to afford rent either. We had nightmares about being thrown out in the streets with our five kids. Mysteriously the money appeared, enough to pay the mortgage until I was able to find a job. It was only later we found out that it was Father Campbell who had sent the money through one of my cousins whom he knows, and that he had sold his own car to raise the money. I'll never be able to pay him back, but I was told he didn't want it back. You don't come across people like that very often. Some people say he's tough when it comes to Church matters, but I can't imagine it."

By that time the two were approaching the entrance to the church. The street was still crowded. Uniformed policemen had difficulty keeping clear the walkway from the rectory so the procession could advance in orderly fashion. As the bells tolled in powerful bursts of joyful exuberance, the procession emerged from the rectory. First came the deacon bearing the Book of the Gospels, its gold and jeweled cover glistening in the sun. He was followed by altar boys and girls, then the part of the choir that was not already in the church, and ranks of clergy of various denominations, including Orthodox bishops in their unusual trappings. Then emerged the consecrating bishops and Archbishop O'Connell from the neighboring archdiocese. Last was the bishop-elect, David Campbell, with his two assisting priests.

Father Campbell was impressive in his priestly robes. He was tall and not powerfully built, but scholarly-looking. His walnut-colored hair was slightly wavy, and his metal-rimmed glasses accented his intellectual appearance.

His long, tapering fingers moved gracefully as he waved to people lining the procession route, a shy smile etching his finely chiseled features. His thin face showed the strain he had been under since his call to the bishopric. A long, thin nose of precise proportion was set between warm, penetrating brown eyes that smiled easily, betraying a kind peacefulness beneath the surface. His look seemed to linger rather than move rapidly, hinting at a thoughtfulness that absorbed everything, weighing carefully, never forgetting. David was not a simple man. What appeared on the surface of his life gave no indication of the wholly different world that existed beneath, into which he would not allow even his most intimate friends to penetrate.

As the procession moved into the church, working its way up the aisle, the organ music stopped and the choir intoned the processional, magnified by the almost two thousand happy voices that filled the vast, vaulting sanctuary. Many of the bishops were smiling to people they recognized as they walked up the aisle. The bishop-elect, his hands folded with palms pressed together, seemed unaware of anything around him. His eyes looked straight ahead but not seeing, as if he were absorbed in thoughts of things far away, or deep within.

As the procession approached the sanctuary, only the officiating bishops and their assistants entered, together with the bishop-elect and his two assisting priests. He was seated before the altar facing the congregation.

"In the name of the Father, and of the Son, and of the Holy Spirit," the archbishop intoned. The congregation roared its "Amen." "My brothers and sisters," he continued, "we have come here today from many places and many backgrounds, but all as God's children. He is very much present here with us as we prepare for the consecration of our friend David as bishop. As we call upon our Father to witness and consecrate what we do, we humbly acknowledge our own sins and failings, and beg for His forgiveness. Lord, have mercy. Christ, have mercy. Lord, have mercy."

The Liturgy of the Word continued, and after the

Gospel, the ordination of the bishop-elect took place. The choir sang *"Veni, Creator Spiritus"*: "Come, Creator Spirit, touch the minds of these your children, fill with your heavenly grace these hearts you have created."

During the singing of the hymn, David was led by his assistants to the place of consecration.

"Most Reverend Father," one of the priests addressed the archbishop, "the Church of this diocese asks you to ordain this priest, David, for service as bishop."

"Have you the mandate from the Holy See?" the archbishop asked.

"We have."

After the letter was read, the archbishop addressed the whole assembly. "Consider carefully the position in the Church to which our brother is about to be raised. Our Lord Jesus Christ, who was sent by the Father to redeem the human race, in turn sent twelve apostles into the world. These men were filled with the power of the Holy Spirit to preach the Gospel to every race and people into a single flock to be guided in the way of holiness. Because this service was to be until the end of time, the apostles selected others to help them. By the laying on of hands which confers the sacrament in its fullness, the apostles passed on the gift of the Holy Spirit, which they themselves had received from Christ. In that way, by a succession of bishops unbroken from one generation to the next, the powers conferred in the beginning were handed down, and the work of the Savior lives and grows in our time." Then, looking at David, he continued, "You, dear brother, have been chosen by the Lord to guide His people. You have been chosen to serve rather than to rule, and to proclaim the good news of Jesus endlessly. You are called to be a good shepherd in imitation of the Master. Love all those entrusted to you: the poor, the sick, the weak, strangers, and the homeless, as well as those who are rich in the things of this world. May your own life be blameless and a shining reflection of the goodness of Jesus Himself. And may God have mercy on your soul, as you accept this awesome responsibility."

The liturgy, stripped of all the medieval pageantry that had once characterized these ceremonies, was still impressive. The rich traditions of the Church, the unbroken line of priestly power and authority that Jesus had given to His apostles and which He had intended should be passed on forever, were reflected in every facet of the beautiful and timeless rite. David could trace his own spiritual lineage to one of the apostles through the unbroken line of succession. It was a graphic expression of the organic bond between the Church of every age with the living Christ who walked the roads of Palestine.

After all the preliminary interrogations and prayers, the bishops laid their hands on David as he knelt before them. With the Book of the Gospels held above his head, the archbishop recited the prayer of consecration over him: ". . . Father, pour out Your Spirit upon Your chosen, that he may be a shepherd of Your holy flock and a high priest blameless in Your sight. Grant him every power You bestowed upon the apostles themselves, so he may carry on their work in our time. May he be pleasing to You by his gentleness and purity of heart, presenting a fragrant offering to You, through Jesus Your Son."

After the consecration, the symbols of office were presented: the Book of the Gospels, the ring, the miter, and the shepherd's staff. The Mass continued as usual, but when the ceremony ended, thunderous applause spontaneously erupted, attesting to the extraordinary popularity of this quiet and unassuming cleric.

It was difficult for many of David's colleagues to understand the reason for his popularity, since his recent assignments were not high profile situations in which he could cultivate a following. He worked part-time at the chancery, where he had a reputation for exact observance of Church law. When people called for help with difficult predicaments, he would always listen, but if help demanded bending any of the rules or countermanding canon law, he could be uncompromising. Many people left hurt and more alienated from the Church than before they came to see him. He could be cold and detached when applying the law. The book was everything. That was most probably the reason he was selected to be bishop. He was predictable and dedicated to what was expected of a loyal Church official.

Two women on the chancery staff summed it up as they gossiped while exiting the church. "How do you explain why there are so many unusual people here today?" Joan Carey asked the chancery receptionist, Marilyn Cotugno. Joan was not one of David's most avid fans. "I'll never get over the way he handled my sister's case when she came to him for advice. I thought that of all the priests at the chancery he would be the one most likely to understand her problem. She came home that night crying, vowing she'd never go to church again. I certainly can't see why people think he's so great. Charlie Mayberry was really upset when David's appointment was announced."

"Don't you think that was because he was jealous? Charlie would have loved to have been made bishop," Marilyn interjected.

"That's possible, but Charlie still doesn't think much of David. He's forever criticizing the way he does things and tried to get him appointed pastor just to get him out of the chancery."

Marilyn liked David and wasn't about to let him be hacked at like this even by her friend. "Well, how do you explain the unusual demonstration of affection today?"

"It's beyond me," Joan answered with a look of bewilderment.

"Perhaps it's from people he works with in his free time," Marilyn put in by way of David's defense. "He does have a reputation for quietly working with all kinds of people, non-Catholics included, and for helping people in trouble. I'll never forget the time he took a part-time job on the docks to earn money to buy food for poor families whose income was so little they could hardly survive. My Jewish friends tell me he goes to their synagogue on Friday nights and says his prayers in Hebrew. Even Muslims like him because he fights with immigration on behalf of family members who had been refused entrance into the country on technicalities. You have to admit he's shrewd the way he uses his contacts. I think that's the real David. What we see in the chancery is the company man who always goes by the book, but that's what's expected of him. I'm sure that's the reason he was made bishop, because he was such a good company man. I think we are really going to get a surprise once he gets a chance to be himself."

Marilyn wasn't far from wrong. It was for the thorough and faithful performance of his official responsibilities that David was now being rewarded by the Church.

The ceremony over, the clergy met at the cathedral rectory briefly, then departed for the civic center for the lavish dinner and gala festivities. The governor was there, along with other state officials and dignitaries from faraway places. People obviously thought much of and expected much from this new celebrity; they felt honored to have been invited to his ordination.

David was unusually quiet at the dinner, although he talked warmly and politely to everyone, graciously expressing his gratitude to each for attending and for the good wishes. As the day wore on one could see the strain in his face and sense his need to be away from the crowd, alone.

That is just what he did when it all ended. A man other than David might have preferred further celebration and camaraderie; but after thanking the archbishop and all the other bishops, he left for his home to spend the night alone.

After falling into a deep sleep on the couch for a few hours, he woke up and had a drink. Then he went to his room and knelt at his prie-dieu, which faced a stark reproduction of the Crucifixion by El Greco. As he knelt, his face resting in his hands, he became absorbed in his thoughts.

"O, my God, what have I done? What have I taken upon myself? For years I sensed this day would come, and as it approached I became more and more fearful. If only they had known the visions, the thoughts, the conflicts that haunted me, they would never have done this. Now I am here and there is no turning back. For the rest of my life I must live this calling, not as others see it, but as I, under the light of Your grace, understand it. Help me, God, I am frightened. Jesus, Good Shepherd, teach me. I will follow You faithfully wherever You may lead. Only guide me, I am afraid."

David prayed intermittently. At intervals his mind wandered. He did not know whether he had fallen off to sleep and had dreamed dreams, or whether in his openness to God, God was speaking to him.

One dream—or revelation or vision—was particularly disturbing. A woman, troubled and crying, a look of haunting anguish on her face, was pointing at David. "You have done this to me. You have done this to me. I trusted you as I trusted God and you turned me away. Now see my children. Look at them, see what has happened to them, and all because of you." Two children appeared in the dream, boys in their late teens, angry children, throwing stones at a church and turning to David with the accusation, "Righteous priest, god without a heart. If that's what he's like, you keep him. We'll have none of him."

David recognized the woman and the boys. She had come to him years ago with a problem. Her husband had left her and abandoned the children. In her loneliness, she had found a man who cared for her and was devoted to the children. They in turn loved him as a father. The woman had been raised in a rigidly traditional family and was troubled over the affair. She decided to tell David the whole story. David told her that her relationship with the man was sinful and that it could not continue; it could not but do spiritual damage to the children. In discussing the possibility of marrying the man, David advised that both their previous marriages be annulled. When that proved impossible because of insurmountable obstacles, he insisted she end the relationship and raise the children as best she could by herself, promising that God would take care of her. Her upbringing had instilled in her enough loyalty to the Church to follow his instructions. She broke off the relationship and tried to make the best of the difficult situation. It proved too much. The children were heartbroken because they missed this man who had become a father to them. The mother's own life began to fall apart, and in her anguish, she turned against God.

The dream epitomized the cruelty of a law heartlessly imposed with no feeling for the lives of those involved. The Good Shepherd certainly would not have acted that way. The Pharisees, maybe, and the Scribes, but not the Good Shepherd who cared for the sheep. "The law was made for man and not man for the law," he once said when he justified a shocking thing King David once did because his troops were hungry. Jesus' justification for David's violation of the law was that there was a human need.

The events of this night were things the new bishop had never experienced before. His prayer had always been detached, quiet, uneventful. What was happening now was shaking him to the depths of his soul. When he periodically came to, he would look up at the figure of Christ and in a cold sweat murmur, "O, my God, no, no. I haven't been that way. Have I really hurt those people that deeply? I was only trying to fulfill my responsibility to the Church in insisting that people observe the letter of the law." The guilt was unbearable, the vivid revelation of his whole past life being acted out in comparison to the Good Shepherd. As saintly as David's life as a priest had been, in contrast to the beauty of Christ's relationship with God's children it was appalling. The law had always been the basis of religion as applied to life. It was so obvious the way Jesus excoriated the Scribes and Pharisees and chief priests that that was not the way. Yet that is what it had become, the exact observance of law no matter what the damage to God's children.

David's soul was seared by the revelations he suffered that night. He would never again be the same. He could never see people in the same way as before. His whole vision of the Church would be forever transformed. He had been touched to the core of his being.

It was far into the night, perhaps just before dawn, when David was almost completely consumed with weariness, that a strange thing occurred. David had slipped from the prie-dieu and fallen on the floor. Bent over, crying uncontrollably from the frightful experiences of the night, suddenly he felt a strange calm. He knelt up straight and looked above him. His face grew peaceful.

His eyes were not looking at anything in the room, yet he was seeing something that was deeply affecting him. As all the horrible nightmares passed, David could see a man walking across a field. Of ordinary build, he was dressed in modern clothes, khaki-colored trousers and a brown pullover shirt open at the collar. He had strong but gentle, clean-shaven features. His hair was full and wavy, but not long. His gentle hazel eyes seemed to penetrate David's soul. The man said nothing, but his presence filled David with a deep sense of peace. David immediately recognized him as a man he thought he had seen in the last pew during his consecration. The panic, the fear, the trauma of the past hours disappeared. The presence of this man, whoever he was, healed David's soul like a soothing balm and seemed to give meaning to all that had taken place that night.

The dreamlike vision passed. The rays of the morning sun began to fill the room. Morning had finally come after a night that had seemed endless.

David was drained of every last drop of energy, but he felt strangely alive and invigorated. He dropped onto the bed, fully dressed, intending to rest briefly, and fell into a deep sleep.

CHAPTER

2

THE LOUD BANGING on
the front door finally roused David from his deep sleep.
It was Father Jim Mohr, his new secretary. Jim was a
young fellow, full of life, the epitome of efficiency. He
was told to be at David's at eight o'clock, and at the dot
of eight he was there ringing the bell, to no avail. Banging on the door was the only way he could get any action.

David answered the door red-eyed and in something
of a stupor, but with a smile and in a good-natured
mood. "C'mon in, Jim. I guess I overslept on my first
day. What a way to start my new job!"

"I'm sure everyone will understand," Jim responded.
"Yesterday was a long day. You should have taken the
day off to rest, anyway."

"Give me a few minutes while I shower and get into
shape. I'll be right out, then we can offer Mass together.
Have you had breakfast?"

"No, just a cup of coffee, but I'll be all right," Jim
replied shyly, embarrassed that his new boss would so
honor him as to invite him to offer Mass and eat with
him.

They offered Mass at the dining room table, a simple
rite, reminiscent of the Breaking of Bread in the early

Church. After Mass, David cooked breakfast for the two of them, then they started on their way to the chancery.

"Don't you think you should have taken a few days off before you start working?" Jim asked respectfully.

"No, I'm anxious to get started. I may take some time later in the week, but I want to get a handle on things."

The chancery was a stately château, befitting a diplomat's residence, with a courtyard in front of the elegant entrance. Jim parked the car in the courtyard, in the spot marked BISHOP, and the two men entered the building. The staff was standing around waiting for the new boss, not knowing what to expect. Everyone sensed he could go either way, doing everything according to the book or following his own ideas and charting an entirely new course. No one knew where he stood, either, which made them all apprehensive. It was impossible to read this man with any degree of certainty, even though they had worked with him daily for years. Anyone with any degree of discernment could sense this was a very complex individual, who may appear warm and caring on the outside, but underneath God only knew what transpired.

As David entered, they all clapped and welcomed him enthusiastically. He gave each of them a hug and thanked them for their cordial welcome, telling them he would like to see everyone in the conference room at ten o'clock. Then he walked to his office, followed by Father Jim and two secretaries.

There was already a number of calls to be returned, a full-page list lying on his desk. He glanced at it, put it aside, and sat down behind his desk. Father Jim sat discreetly off to the side. The two secretaries had notes in their hands with requests for appointments. He took the notes and, after exchanging a few pleasantries, said he would like a few minutes to compose himself and prepare some comments for.the meeting at ten o'clock. Father Jim and the two secretaries left.

The meeting started promptly at ten. The staff consisted of approximately twenty people, priests, sisters, and lay people. Standing at the lectern, dressed in a black suit and Roman collar, with the gold pectoral cross resting over his heart, David began his first official act as ordinary of the diocese.

"Fathers, ladies, gentlemen: First, I would like to thank all of you for being so gracious over the past several weeks. I know it has not been easy doing your regular work as well as all the extra work demanded by the preparations for the ordination and the festivities. I am grateful to each of you. I realize I should have taken a few days off to get my bearings, but I am anxious to get started. I have been doing so much soul-searching lately that I would never have been able to rest if I had taken the time off. It is better to get started and set things in motion first.

"Last night I spent the whole night in prayer; not talking to God but listening. It was the most stirring and frightening moment of my life, even more moving than yesterday's beautiful ceremony. At the end, I found a peace I had never known, and a sense of direction and purpose that had previously eluded me. Although we have worked together for years in this place, and I have a reputation for being solidly stuck in concrete, I have long sensed that if God came into this place, He would say the same things to us that He said to the Scribes and Pharisees."

There was a stunned silence. At the odious comparison, some of the older officials winced, while others felt uncomfortable. But David continued. "During the ceremony yesterday, the archbishop kept talking about the Good Shepherd, and about the bishop being a shepherd. That hit home forcefully, and for the first time I realized bishops are no longer shepherds. Other than a few pastoral letters on rare occasions, we rarely teach or talk to our people about the devastating problems facing them today, the frightful crises that are crushing their lives. We may follow the lead of others in social movements, but we are certainly not the fearless, outspoken leaders we should be. For all practical purposes bishops have become like mini-governors, ruling a vast conglomerate of agencies and offices and schools, while priests in the parishes are out on the front lines bearing the heat of the day and carrying the real burdens that weigh heavily on today's Church."

David could see some of the staff was becoming visibly upset, so he decided to ask for their reactions and suggestions.

"I realize that what I am saying may come as a shock, and I am open to suggestions. Does anyone have any thoughts about what I have just said?"

A older gentleman, Bob Werlin, who had worked as a bookkeeper in the chancery for years, put up his hand. After David recognized him, he asked, "The Church has been doing things in the same way for hundreds of years—why would anyone want to change that? The Church has been successful. It has continued to grow. Why disturb a good thing?"

"I suppose we have all had different experiences, Bob. In your work you don't deal with people in the same way some others do. I have come across many hurting and troubled people in the Church who need healing. A good shepherd will do all he can to heal. Changes in canon law have not lightened burdens for our people, nor for the priests. They have made workloads in the parishes almost unbearable and have not addressed those things that are hurting so many of our people."

"How are our people hurting?" the man asked, unable to comprehend what David was talking about.

"Many people are troubled with guilt," David answered.

"Well, why don't they just straighten their lives out? Then they won't need to feel guilty," Bob objected.

"It isn't that simple," David replied. "The guilt is not necessarily from things they can do anything about, like the guilt of parents who have tried so hard to raise their children conscientiously only to see them go wrong, or the guilt of married people who have been indoctrinated with the idea that divorce is evil, then after years of marriage must face exactly that if a spouse leaves.

"The problem of divorce and remarriage troubles me. Almost half of our people have no hope of ever seeing their marriages recognized by the Church. They are technically cut off from the life of the Church and the sacraments. That is not right. The Good Shepherd never cut Himself off from people who were hurting and had difficulties with the law. We say they are sinners and

unworthy to receive Christ. That is arrogant and hypocritical. That was the way the Pharisees treated people, and Jesus condemned them for it."

"Well, if they are living in sin, why should the
Church mollycoddle them?" Bob persisted.

"It is not a matter of mollycoddling, Bob. It is a
matter of not assuming the role of Christ as Judge. We
are shepherds and gentle guides, not moral policemen.
Judgment belongs to God. When you have over thirty-
five percent of our people living in violation of canon
law, could it not just be that it is our law that may be
unrealistic? Is it Christlike to cut all those people off
from Christ, because they don't observe Church law?
And if they did apply for annulments, how large a staff
would you need to annul five million marriages? Even
financially it is not practical. We have to search for
other ways."

Another of David's big concerns was the shortage of
priests, and he now wanted to discuss that issue.

"Our priests are dwindling in numbers. In fifteen
years most of our churches will be without priests. That
is not God's fault. It is our fault. We are not accepting
many whom God has called because His choices do not
conform to our job description. So we will in a short time
be faced with a priestless Church, at a time when people
need good, healthy priests more than ever.

"These are just a few of the problems we must address. I realize we can't solve them overnight, but we
can start. The first decision I want to share with you
this morning is not something I have taken lightly. It
was after much soul-searching and prayer. It is the role
of bishop to be shepherd and father of Jesus' flock. This

I intend to be, to the best of my ability. I do not intend to be chief administrator to all our agencies and schools. I don't feel that is what Jesus intended for his apostles, so I would like the chancellor and his assistants to make plans to turn all the agencies and charitable and social programs over to the laypeople. They are to be totally separated from the chancery. The laypeople are more than competent to handle these matters."

David paused at this point as if looking for comments. The chancellor, Father Charles Mayberry, asked how they could cut the Catholic schools off from the chancery's oversight.

"The schools are a separate situation," David said. "I have been talking to directors of some of the national corporations in our area about adopting our schools and working with us. They can use the schools as training centers for their operations so our graduates will not only qualify for college, but those not going to college will receive a highly technical training that will prepare them for jobs in industry upon graduation. Our schools, public as well as private, need this kind of cooperation with industry. The response has been overwhelmingly positive.

"My own role will be more modest. I will go from parish to parish helping the pastors and priests and people to develop communities of caring Christians. The funds we take in here will be used to assist parishes in setting up programs to help their own people. I envision each area in the diocese having its own nursing home and apartments for the elderly so they don't have to leave friends and loved ones in search of care far away. I envision clinics in rural areas where people can receive immediate aid in medical emergencies, and hospices placed discreetly around the diocese where troubled young people and abused married people can come for help.

"These are the concerns that are uppermost in my mind. I share them with you today, so you can sense the direction our work will be taking in the future. I expect you to discuss these concerns among yourselves and be able to offer me practical suggestions and advice as to approaches we might use in implementing these ideas. Does anyone have any questions?"

David waited, fully expecting a barrage of objections. There was nothing but silence. He didn't know how to interpret it, whether positively or negatively. Perhaps they were too overwhelmed and stunned by what he had said.

As soon as David dismissed the staff, the chancellor went immediately to his office and picked up his private phone. The call was to the archbishop. Even though the archbishop had no direct authority over another diocese, his influence was enormous, particularly with Rome and with the papal pronuncio in Washington. His nod was critical in the selection of bishops. The chancellor was the archbishop's source of information on everything that transpired in the diocese. This conversation would overheat the telephone lines.

"Archbishop?"

"Yes."

"This is Charles Mayberry."

"Right on the job first day, I see."

"Yes, and do I have news. This man is off the wall. We just had our first conference. You wouldn't believe what he intends to do. He told us he wants us to dismantle the whole diocesan structure, including the school system, and all the agencies. I think he's flipped. He placed me in charge of the operation and I have to come up with the practical plans for implementing all of this, and in the process put myself out of a job. What do you think I should do?"

"First of all, calm down. His first conference is just so much idealism. It will pass. In the meantime, just keep your eyes open and see if he really intends to act on these things. Just what is it he wants to accomplish?"

"Well, for starters, he said he wants us to turn all the agencies over to the lay people. The schools he intends to turn over to industry. Imagine, the very first day, no less. You would think he would wait a year or at least a few months. But the very first day! I can't believe it."

"Calm down, Charles, calm down. He'll realize how impractical these things are. He'll back off. We would all like to get rid of these headaches, but it's not possible in the first place and too radical to even consider. Don't worry. He'll soon be busy with real problems and won't even have time to work on this. Keep me informed."

"Thank you, Bishop," Charles replied and hung up.

As soon as Charles put down the phone there was a knock on his door. "Come in," Charles called out.

It was David. He had seen Charles make a beeline for his room after the meeting. David had known for a long time that Charles had a direct line to the archbishop's office and that everything he did and said would be immediately reported. David had considered dropping Charles as chancellor but decided to let events take their course. Even Judas was a necessity in Jesus' accomplishment of His Father's work.

"Come in, Bishop," Charles said with a sheepish look as he stood up. The bishop entered and sat down.

"Charles, I know I may have come off pretty strong in the conference, but it is because I feel so strongly about all the things I discussed. I realize it may seem radical, and there will be a lot of opposition, but I hope I can count on you. You know more than anyone else about the operation around here, and you have your fingers on all the right buttons. I hope I can depend on you for help. It won't be easy, and I won't be able to do it without you. Can I count on you?"

Charles was caught off guard. He hoped the bishop hadn't overheard his conversation with the archbishop; but there was no reason he should have. "Bishop, you know you have my support. What you proposed was quite bold, but with everyone's cooperation, there's no reason why it shouldn't work. I'll do my part."

"Thanks, Charles. I knew I could count on you, even though the changes will affect you more than anyone else here. I would appreciate it if you could help me with the proposal to shift the focus onto the parishes. The hardest job will be moving the parishes in the direction we would like."

"That's going to be tough, Bishop. You know the pastors. They are not about to accept interference in the way they've been accustomed to doing things. However, I'll do what I can to help."

By that time, it was almost noon. The bishop and the staff gathered in the dining room and ate together. A few of the lay help went out to the local deli for lunch.

3

DAVID worked the first days at the chancery setting agenda and formulating policy before taking the rest of the week off. He had decided to make the cathedral his base of operations by offering Mass and preaching each Sunday as his way of fulfilling his role as shepherd and chief teacher of the diocese, and issued a news release to that effect.

There was need for the Church to be renewed, he felt, and it wasn't renewal in ritual or in things superficial that concerned him, but renewal at the core, a revival of faith itself. Many Christians today were not even sure who Jesus was. David was disillusioned at the shallowness of the renewal as he saw it in both Protestant and Catholic churches, based as it was merely on a dilettante approach to Scripture, liturgy, and social involvement. There was more to Christianity than Scripture or liturgy. If the Holy Spirit had been guiding the Church for the past two thousand years, as Jesus promised He would, then the Church should have advanced significantly in its understanding of the message of Jesus. That should be reflected in the beliefs and culture of the Church. To reject all that the Spirit had taught and inspired for two thousand years and go back to the cradle of the written word did not make sense.

Using Scripture as the inspired word of God, as David had done all his life—a vehicle for developing a deeper understanding of the mind of Christ and the way God works in our lives—was important to him, and God spoke to him powerfully through His word. But God certainly could not be limited to guiding His Church merely through the written word, which He never told anyone to write in the first place. "Go and teach," was Jesus' command, ". . . and I will be with you until the end of time . . . and will send the Holy Spirit to bring back to your minds all that I have taught you."

David believed that God worked continually through individuals. In the Old Testament he worked through the magisterium of the high priests, the Scribes, and the Pharisees, yet still called prophets to stir the minds and hearts of religious leaders and the people when they wandered from the path he clearly marked out for them. It will always be that way. How can anyone dare to muzzle God and say how He must work and through whom He must speak? David was convinced that the real renewal of Christianity had yet to begin, and intended to leave himself open so God could use him in whatever way He pleased.

David was also convinced that God had spoken to him the night of his consecration and had no doubt that God was using that frightful and comforting experience to open his soul to a whole new understanding of the meaning of the Good Shepherd and the direction God intended the Church should take in our times. Speaking in the cathedral every week would provide a vehicle for God's message and a steady diet of solid teaching for the people who desperately needed thoughtful guidance through the crises they faced in their everyday lives. With careful planning his talks could be televised over the commercial channels and could reach every corner of his diocese, the churched and the unchurched. This role as teacher was the one great bishops of the past delighted in most. Augustine was moved to accept Christ by hearing the sermons of Bishop Ambrose in Milan. Augustine himself preached unceasingly, when he finally found God after a life of sin, giving not only Sunday sermons but seasonal instructions to the people of his diocese. It is unfortunate the custom had fallen into disuse, David felt. As a result people suffer serious malnutrition in their spiritual lives. The Church itself as a force in society suffers.

As soon as David left for his few days off, the chancery hummed like an agitated hornet's nest. His announcement had proved traumatic. Staff's first concern was whether they would still have a job. Assured they would, they felt secure enough to discuss the proposal more calmly. The hard-core traditionalists were close to apoplexy and made no secret of their resentful anger at having their whole secure world shattered in one rash, ill-conceived scheme on the part of an immature bishop who had no respect for the past.

The following weekend David offered Mass at the cathedral. The news media had done him the courtesy of announcing that he would be officiating there regularly, so a good crowd attended the service. For his first sermon he told the people that before all else he wanted to be accessible to them. It might prove impossible before very long, but he wanted to at least start out that way. Previous bishops had been accessible to a point, but only to those carefully screened. He mentioned that he was aware of how much the people were hurting in these very complicated and troubled times, and that he wanted to help heal their many wounds and bruised souls. He also informed them that he would be speaking in the cathedral each week and hoped large crowds would attend. There were so many concerns he wanted to discuss with them, including the severe crisis of faith in the Church and the devastating moral issues of the day. He wanted more than anything to be a real bishop to them, a true good shepherd to the flock that God had entrusted to him. He ended in a very humble tone by asking for their prayers that God would teach him how to be a good bishop.

The second week ended up being a seventy-hour week. It started out smoothly and quietly enough, with David meeting with the heads of the various diocesan agencies, the diocesan school board, and school officials, sharing with them his vision for the future. They were polite but dumbfounded. To their objections that his plan could spell doom to the whole complex of charitable programs, he respectfully disagreed. The diocese could no longer afford to maintain an ever-growing bureaucracy without draining the parishes so there would be nothing left for them to do the real work of the Church at the proper level, that of the parish. The parishes had to flourish. Programs for the people had to be there. The agencies could perhaps help the parishes set up and maintain the programs they needed and could shift the emphasis of their work in that direction. Diocesan monies would be distributed to the parishes so the people could be convinced that the Church was concerned about them and serious in its willingness to support and help them.

The school officials were worried about turning the schools over to industry. David told them it was a matter he had been looking into for a long time, and that he had talked to business leaders about his ideas. Most of the children were not being prepared for life after graduation. And since industry was hard pressed for skilled labor, it really should share the burden of educating the young. The companies are the ones who would benefit from their training later on, and it was to their advantage to provide a good education for them, David pointed out. The diocese would still provide the teachers who would instill Christian values in the students, but the partnership with industry would offer a comprehensive technical education particularly for those students who would not be college bound.

There wasn't really much for those in attendance to object to. The bishop's mind was obviously made up. To object might jeopardize their jobs, they feared. Clearly, their new bishop was proving to be unlike any they had had.

Perhaps David should have been more prudent in the beginning of his pontificate. He hadn't considered the innate insecurity of the people who surrounded him. Nor could he imagine how the heads of all the agencies would spend half their nights criticizing the half-baked ideas of their new bishop. The chancellor was the key to the percolating opposition. They all knew where he stood, so they funneled all their objections and hostility through him. He was only too willing to listen, and pass them on to the proper places.

The second week at the chancery seemed routine enough on the surface, but underneath a drama was already beginning to unfold, so subtle it completely escaped the awareness of the main character. David went home each night feeling secure that his vision of the Church and his role as bishop were being well received and had the support of all his staff. Or, perhaps, in his attempt to be genuinely Christlike, he was intentionally overlooking the meanness surrounding him. Still, two simultaneous conflicts were developing, one on the surface of daily events, the other a devious drama obvious only to the participants themselves, as they wrote their own script.

CHAPTER 4

AT HOME in the evening, David pored over the map of the diocese. It was a sprawling territory covering five large counties, one consisting of the metropolitan area, with its core city and suburbs. This was home to a number of industries, some large national corporations with international subsidiaries. David's diocese formed a good cross-section of society, some well-to-do, including top officers in the corporations, most middle-class, and a good number of genuinely poor people. David could feel close to them all and had real friends in each group.

Four of the counties hugged the river and stretched out into the hill country that was covered with lakes and resorts and, in the winter, prosperous ski centers. In those out-of-the-way areas the people were not wealthy. Of all the members of the diocese they more than anyone needed the assistance of their bishop. As David looked over the map, he could see that one by one the churches in those outlying areas had closed from lack of priests. The previous bishop had sent sisters and deacons to these places to celebrate liturgical services, but they were no substitute for their own priest.

As David studied the map, analyzing each area and each parish, trying to picture the real-life situation in each place, his imagination began to work. He realized the people in the isolated areas needed priests more than people in the cities, who had more tangible and ready supports for their faith, like easy access to diocesan agencies and programs. But in the rural areas they lacked the services and trained personnel to help stimulate interest and involvement in their religion to keep the faith alive. David immediately thought of the many priests in the diocese who had left their priesthood to marry. They were good men for the most part, some of them the best. They had certainly been called by God to the priesthood, but just as certainly had not been called to celibacy. David was convinced these men still had a vocation. What a waste they were not allowed to use their priesthood! How these people in the rural areas could benefit from the presence of these dedicated men! He stopped there. He had made enough radical changes already. No one would be prepared for what he was thinking, so he put the idea out of his mind.

Each area of the diocese had different problems. David's years in the chancery made him aware of how much had to be done to answer the needs of the people. As he scanned the map, he began to realize how widespread the crises were, and an unusual anger arose within as he thought of how unrealistic former officials had been in responding to—or, to be more honest, ignoring—the desperate needs of the people.

He determined to do something, but what? He didn't know. Besides, it was getting late, and he was tired from confronting so many problems so quickly in the first few days of his new work. He folded the map, said his prayers, and retired for the night.

The next day he went to the chancery early. There was an elderly nun already waiting for him. She was a short, stocky woman in her eighties, wearing an old-fashioned habit.

"Good morning, Sister," David greeted her warmly. He noted her well-pressed, neatly starched habit. "Your habit brings back a lot of memories of sisters teaching me religion when I went to school. I miss seeing them lately."

"Good morning, Bishop. I appreciate your taking the time to see me. My name is Sister Veronica, and I came because I have a problem that has been torturing me for the longest time."

"Come into my office and tell me about it," David said as he ushered her into his office and offered her his own armchair. The nun sat down, and David took the less comfortable seat next to her.

"Bishop, I am old and was brought up in the old school. It is very difficult for me to adjust to all the changes."

"Don't you worry yourself about all those things. Changes are made for the young generation who find it impossible to understand the old ways. But there is nothing wrong with the old ways, and if you feel comfortable with them then you stay with them in good conscience, as long as you respect the feelings of others in your community."

"Well, Bishop, the thing that is really bothering me is the vow of poverty. We were taught many years ago that the vow of poverty meant that you gave up all worldly possessions. Now the new rules stipulate you can keep the gifts people give you and save it for your vacation, and also use the money to buy presents for family and friends if you like. That troubles me."

"How much do you have saved, Sister?"

"Forty-five dollars, and it will increase as the months go by."

"Well, I think the change in procedure stems from the fact that convent treasurers had problems when everyone wanted to go on vacation and all the income had already been spent on bills. So, to make things simpler and make sure there was enough money for everyone's vacation, the sisters were charged with banking their own money. Since you were given the permission to save the money, you are not breaking your vow, so don't you worry about it."

"But what about the buying of presents, Bishop?"

"Sister, I am sure it doesn't amount to large sums of money. If what you buy are gifts that are mere tokens of friendship, I am sure there is nothing wrong with that. If you spend large sums, then you will know that it is not right. So don't worry yourself about it, Sister. I can tell you are conscientious."

"Thank you so much, Bishop. You don't know how you have relieved my mind. That has been bothering me for so long."

As the nun got up to leave, David rose with her and led her into the dining room. "Would you have a cup of tea with me, Sister Veronica?" The nun was too flattered to say no. After they finished, David walked the sister to the door.

The next person to see David was a young mother by the name of Janet Maynard. She was upset. "Bishop, I don't know where to start. I have four children. The oldest is six years old. The youngest is only three months. I tried to arrange to have the baby baptized, but the pastor refused. He told me I didn't go to church and that I was living in sin because I was not married in the Church."

"Janet, do you go to church?"

"Yes, I do, Bishop, though not very often. It is difficult with so many little ones. I go maybe once a month, or six weeks, and I bring the children with me, so they can learn about Mass."

"Is it true you did not marry in the Church?"

"Yes, it is, Bishop, but I had no choice. My husband doesn't like the Catholic Church, and wouldn't hear of getting married in our Church."

"Do you teach the children about God?"

"Yes, Bishop, I say their prayers with them every night, and tell them stories about Jesus when I tuck them in."

"What is your pastor's name?"

"Father O'Donnell."

David called his secretary on the intercom and directed her to call Father O'Donnell for him. In no time he was on the phone.

"Hello, Bill, how are things up in the valley?"

"Fine, Bishop. That was a beautiful ceremony they arranged for your ordination. We are all happy for you."

"Bill, do you know a lady by the name of Janet Maynard?"

"Yes, I do, Bishop. She came in to see me last week."

"Well, she is here in the office now, concerned about getting her baby baptized. Do you know if she goes to church?"

"Yes, I do see her here occasionally."

"About how often?"

"Maybe once a month or so."

"Does she bring the children?"

"Yes, usually."

"Are you aware that her husband has a dislike for the Catholic Church?"

"No, I didn't know that, Bishop. That explains a lot."

"Do you know of any justifiable reason why her baby should not be baptized, Bill?"

"Putting it the way you do, Bishop, I guess the woman is doing about all that can be expected. Why don't you have her stop in to have a talk with me? I'm sure we can work it out."

"Thanks, Bill, and while I have you on the phone, would you mind if I stopped out and had dinner with you some evening?"

"Not at all. In fact, I'd be honored."

"I'll have my secretary make the arrangements. Take care, Bill, and thanks for your help."

"You're welcome, Bishop," the pastor said as they both hung up.

"Well, Janet, it looks as if you don't have a problem. Father would like you to stop in and have a chat with him. He doesn't see any reason why you can't work out the arrangements."

"Oh, Bishop, thank you so much. You don't know how happy you have made me. I promise I will do all I can to be a good mother to the children and that they will learn all they should about God and their religion."

"I'm sure you will, Janet. Now go in peace and enjoy the beautiful day," he said to her as he walked her to the door.

David was upset that a priest would refuse to baptize a baby. He understood the problems pastors were having with people who never went to church, never lifted a finger to help with things that had to be done around the parish, never offered any support with the severe financial burdens of the parish, then wanted the red carpet treatment for their baptisms and weddings. It was understandable that pastors felt used by these people, but it was crude and hurtful for a man of God to retaliate in such a vindictive fashion. That could not be allowed. David took out his notebook and jotted down a memo to write a letter to all the priests, giving detailed guidelines for just such situations.

The rest of the day was routine. Lunchtime was a little more relaxed than during the first week. The staff was still apprehensive but felt slightly more comfortable. David treated them all as if they were his friends and gave not the slightest hint he knew what was transpiring behind the scenes. He, too, had his friends at the archbishop's office—one of his old classmates, no less, who kept him informed every time the chancellor contacted the archbishop.

The rest of the afternoon continued calm. David decided to leave early. It was a beautiful day and a perfect time to work in his garden, turning over the soil to ready it for early planting.

The ride home was short. David lived in the house

his mother and father left to him. The garden was at the side of the house, in slightly from the sidewalk and protected by a white picket fence. David enjoyed working in the dirt. It made him feel down-to-earth and humble, a real part of life. Neighbors passing by enjoyed seeing a priest work, and even men who didn't go to church would stop and exchange pleasantries with this casual, likable priest.

David had been working in the garden for only a few minutes when a strange thing happened. A stranger walked up the street. As he approached, David happened to look up, noticed him, and immediately turned white. The man looked over at David and smiled, saying "Hello." Still paralyzed from the shock, David hardly reacted, other than to say a perfunctory hello in return.

The stranger was the same person David had seen in the vision the night of his consecration, and he was wearing the exact same clothes. He walked over to the fence and extended his hand to David. David walked over and shook his hand.

"David, I am Joshua. I was walking by and thought I'd stop and say hello. I see you are off to a good start with your garden. You should have a good season if there are no late frosts."

After getting over the shock of this stranger knowing his name, David responded. "Yes, that's what I'm hoping, especially since I want to get an early start with melons this year. I've never had any luck with them."

"Real manure and warm ground are the secrets of good melons," Joshua advised. "Your garden is like your work. You don't worry about what you did in your garden last year. That is past. The work you have to do now is all new. Don't put new wine into old wineskins. The Church must break new ground for the future. Old molds are part of the past and are not sacred. New situations need new tools if the Church is to help people through difficult times. Don't be afraid to use your imagination. God will enlighten you. You are the instrument of God. He will guide you."

"Thank you for the advice, Joshua," David replied. "I'll remember it well, and will try to be faithful in listening to God."

With that the stranger left and walked down the street, disappearing in the distance. David watched, still shaken, but also feeling the same peacefulness he experienced the night of the vision. Who was that man? What was he?

5

J OSHUA'S appearance af-
fected David deeply. He spent a good part of the day
trying to understand what it meant. Who was he? Why
was he appearing in his life? Why had he entered his
dreams? When David went back to work in the garden,
he thought of the vision on the night of his ordination
and then about these cryptic messages about his work.
How did this stranger know about him? How did he
know especially the very ideas he was struggling with
while he worked the garden? The few simple suggestions Joshua made were clear answers to the exact problems troubling him. It was baffling. Turning over the
last chunk of earth, David called it quits for the day and
went inside for supper, still unable to shake the troubling thoughts from his mind.

David did his own cooking, the one event he looked
forward to each day. After washing, he prepared his
supper: rice, chicken, and vegetables; simple enough but
nicely flavored. He was a good cook, and his friends
enjoyed coming to his house for supper because they
knew they were in for a treat.

He spent the rest of the evening planning strategy for
rebuilding parish life. It was a new concept and it would

take all his imagination to bring it to life. Any change would have to start with priests. Parishes were large and unwieldy. It was a rare parish that had less than three thousand people. How do you draw so many people into the intimacy of a family? That was what Jesus intended his people become, families caring for one another. First of all, parishes had to have the feeling their bishop cared about them. It is a rare bishop who knows much about his parishes, other than what is picked up by hearsay or rumor. Priests must be able to know their bishop cares and is not just concerned about what they can do to help him. It should be the other way around. Bishops exist for their people and for their communities, not for the network of agencies that absorb most of their time.

To turn parish life, then, the priest was the key. He had to have clear-cut ideals of parish life and be motivated to breathe life into his people. David had to have the support of the priests themselves, otherwise his plans would fail.

Next morning the chancery was astir with gossip by the time David arrived. Father Edmund Marcel, a popular middle-aged priest of the diocese, had requested an urgent meeting with the bishop. Ed had been assistant at one of the large city parishes, worked with the poor, been active in governmental committees, and had a reputation for being an ideal modern priest, the kind the Church needed if it was to survive. Rumor had it that he had been working too much of late with an attractive woman lawyer from the governor's office, and friends of the chancery staff had seen the two of them out to dinner frequently at various restaurants around town.

David arrived on time and saw Ed in the waiting

room. "Ed, what are you doing here so early?" David asked by way of greeting.

"I just had to see you, David. I hope you don't mind my barging in here like this when you probably have a thousand things to do," Ed asked apologetically.

"Not at all. My priests are always my top priority," David answered warmly, immediately sensing the priest was under stress of some sort. "Come into my office and take a seat. I'll be right there as soon as I check in."

The priest stood waiting for David. As soon as he entered the two men sat down and wasted no time on small talk.

"David," Ed started, "I appreciate your seeing me this morning. I really have been miserable lately."

"From all reports you have been doing remarkably well. I don't know of anyone who has any but the nicest comments about you. You would be proud if you heard them all. In fact, one lady said to me just yesterday that you would be a perfect auxiliary bishop for the diocese, and I must say I agreed with her."

"Don't tell me that, David, you make me feel guilty over what I am about to tell you. I haven't been able to sleep in weeks and I've been getting more and more depressed and anxious," Ed said nervously.

"Over what?" the bishop asked.

"David"—Ed paused a long time—"I've fallen in love."

David reached over and put his hand on the priest's shoulder, saying gently, "What's so horrible about that?" He guessed at the priest's anguish over his ecclesiastically fatal crisis.

Ed looked up, astonished. He had expected any number of reactions but certainly not that one. He looked into David's eyes to see if his reaction was honest or contrived. He saw nothing but compassion, no criticism, not even disappointment.

"You mean it doesn't bother you that I've done something to jeopardize my vocation?"

"I don't see love as jeopardizing a priest's vocation. Falling in love enriches a person's ability to understand life. It is something I've thought about for a long time, Ed, and have long since come to grips with it. I am not upset. Go on and tell me about it and about your friend, too. I do care," the bishop finished.

Ed was taken aback by the young bishop's reaction. He was mystified to see such a mature attitude in so young a man. "She is beautiful, David. At least I think she is. She's a lawyer, works on the governor's staff."

"Do I know her?" David interjected.

"Possibly. She said she met you on a number of occasions involving the governor. In fact, you're her idol, which makes me a little jealous. Her name is Maureen Reilly."

"Oh, yes, I do know her," David responded. "She's a sharp lawyer and has a good sense of humor, too. I have to admit, you do have good taste. She *is* beautiful."

"It started out very innocently, while we were working on some proposed legislation. Maureen was the lawyer the governor assigned to work with me. As we worked together I could see what a rare, compassionate person she was, besides being so bright. I invited her out to dinner several times and we got to know each other personally. Each time I was more impressed. I knew I was falling in love with her and tried to fight it, but she meant too much to me to even think of losing her. It may seem corny, David, and I'm sure everyone in the same situation has felt the same way, but I could feel God touching my life in a very personal way, and also a deep sense of peace, and no shame for feeling the way I did."

David listened attentively, saying nothing. He had heard the same story before, had experienced it himself, so he understood. However, as bishop he was not just a spiritual director. This matter now involved the life of the diocese. His approach to this case would set policy and send signals all across the diocese. He had to be judicious.

"I cannot fault you for falling in love, Ed," David said. "It is not something you can't control just by flipping a switch. I know you have always been prudent and conscientious in everything you do, and I have complete confidence that you approached this matter with the same prayerfulness."

"Yes, David, I didn't treat it lightly. You can't imagine how I agonized over it."

"Have you made any decision as to what you would like to do?" David asked him.

"I had been talking to my confessor, and he was quite upset with me, telling me that I was playing with fire—jeopardizing my immortal soul and compromising my commitment to God. He told me to take time off to distance myself from the situation so I could see things more clearly. I tried, but it made the pain all the worse and I missed Maureen more than ever."

"What can I do to help?" David asked, concerned, knowing how much the priest was hurting.

"David, all I can say is that I know I have a vocation

to the priesthood. I have never doubted that, and I know by the way God uses me with people that my work as a priest is effective. I love the priesthood and I love being a priest, but I also realize just as surely that God did not give me the grace of celibacy, and I need Maureen's love to stabilize my life and keep me from falling into sinful ways. I know it would be impossible for me to live without her without it doing serious damage to myself and my work. I have tried, tried, oh, so hard."

"I believe you have, Ed, and again I ask you what I can do. Do you need time off to think and pray over it?"

"No, I've already done that, Bishop. I don't want to give up the priesthood. I know I have a vocation. I also know I need someone to share my life with. That need has haunted my whole life and caused so much pain and unnecessary distraction that it doesn't make sense. I have almost compromised my priesthood a couple of times because of struggling with this problem, and I don't intend to live that way."

"What are you telling me, Ed?" David asked, perplexed.

"Bishop, is there any possibility of my marrying Maureen and remaining a priest?"

"You will always be a priest, you know that, Ed," the bishop answered.

"I know that, David, but I mean working actively as a priest," Ed pressed.

"In canon law there's no way."

"Are there any loopholes?"

"Not that other bishops haven't explored already, and look what happened to them."

"I realize that, but I thought that with a little inge-
nuity . . ."

"In principle I agree with you wholeheartedly. The
two gifts are separate callings. The Holy Spirit can give
the call to the priesthood to whomever He wishes and
the call to celibacy to whomever. As bishops we have to
be sensitive and responsive to however the Holy Spirit
chooses to work. Knowing you personally I know you
have a vocation. Knowing how stable and conscientious
you are I am also convinced of what you have just told
me about not having the call to celibacy. I am willing to
accept that, and I am willing to follow where the Holy
Spirit leads us, but this is the first time as bishop I have
been confronted with this problem. I must admit I am
bewildered as to what to do. You have taken time to
think and pray over it. Now you have to let me have
some time to pray over it, and we'll discuss it in a week
or so. I do want to help, Ed, and I promise I'll do what
I can."

The priest felt assured and deeply relieved that the
bishop didn't castigate him the way his confessor did,
and happy the bishop was so positive. He was not like
those bishops who seem almost personally offended if a
priest develops a problem like this. The two men walked
out of the office, with David resting his hand on Ed's
shoulder in a gesture of comradeship and support.

As soon as Ed left, David telephoned his top canon
lawyer, Dick Franey.

"Dick, I have a real difficult problem on my hands. I
don't know whether we can resolve it, but I'd at least like
to try if it's possible. I'd appreciate it if you could come

over for dinner. I anticipate a long session over this one."

"Can you give me some idea what the problem is about so I can do a little research before I come?" Dick asked, curious as to the nature of this big problem.

"Yes. Ed Marcel just left. He's fallen in love and wants to marry, but also wants to exercise orders, and is insistent about it. There's no way, he says, he is going to deny his priesthood—he has a vocation. I really don't know what to do, but I feel I should back him up since he feels so strongly about it."

"Bishop, I may be a good canon lawyer, but I'm not a miracle worker, and I'm certainly not ready to take on the Vatican. I hope you're not either."

"I know, Dick, and I'm concerned, but my first responsibility is to my priests. They are sacred. Rules are dispensable. People aren't, and I do intend to make a noble effort to work this one out if I can."

"I admire your grit, David, but so early in your episcopate? I'll stick by you if you really want to do it, but it won't be easy."

"Thanks, Dick. Is six o'clock okay for supper? And what would you like?"

"Surprise me. You always concoct a gourmet masterpiece. I just hope you got some bourbon since last time. That's indispensable. The mouthwash you gave me last time was atrocious."

David laughed. "I'll pick some up on the way home. See you then."

David didn't accomplish much else at work that day. He was preoccupied with Ed Marcel. He knew he could not abandon a priest in his predicament who wanted to practice his priesthood. After all, married priests from other denominations are being allowed to enter the Church and function as priests, David reminded himself. To deny the same right to our own is vindictive and unchristian. It is a clear violation of a basic human right. Even Jesus made celibacy optional: "Let him who can take it, take it." He Himself picked married men as His first priests.

David left lunch early and spent the rest of the hour in the cathedral, which was across the street from the chancery. Praying in the dark sanctuary helped David focus his thoughts and feel the tranquillity of God's presence. There was a mysterious intimacy that radiated from the presence of the Eucharist in the tabernacle and offered a soothing balm to troubled souls that could not be found elsewhere. David spent hours this way, and it was a source of tremendous strength and comfort when he was most troubled. Many people find God in nature. David found Him in the Eucharist and while praying in his room. God reveals Himself in different ways to different people. His relationship to each individual is special. That's what is so beautiful about Him; He has a unique relationship with each one, so no one need be jealous of anyone else.

The afternoon went quickly. David left early to shop and prepare for his dinner guest. The cocktail hour and the dinner were to be relaxed, as David made a point of never talking business during meals. He had already prepared the ingredients for supper by the time Dick arrived, so all that remained was the cooking. The meal was an adventure. It was David's recreation preparing something special and enjoying the satisfaction on his guests' faces while they ate.

After supper the two men retired to the den and over several cordials discussed Ed Marcel's problem and how to resolve it if that was possible. Dick was a good canon lawyer. He had studied in Rome, had worked at the Vatican, and had good contacts there he could trust when he needed them. After David's phone call he had spent the rest of the day researching the laws governing such cases, looking for precedents and searching for loopholes, if possible. There were none. Other than just ignoring the law and seeing how long they could get away with it, there was no legal way to skirt the issue. South American bishops had been successful in going that route, and the Vatican seemed to tolerate it, but there were enough radical conservatives in the States who would make an issue of it and put the Vatican on the spot that it seemed unlikely David could get away with it. With that kind of rigidity, it was almost impossible to address serious issues, because facing issues means change, and some people were too much in love with what they were taught in childhood to allow for creative solutions to problems. It had nothing to do with doctrine or even theology, merely customs and Church laws that had meaning at one time but were now archaic.

Dick spent the better part of an hour trying to talk David out of following the South American route. Finally, David agreed that a move like that at this time could be disastrous and would accomplish nothing. To apply for the dispensation from celibacy should, perhaps, be the first step. However, that could take months or years. David had a suggestion.

He had been close to the Pope ever since his seminary days when the Pope was an archbishop and David used to work in his diocese during the summer months. The Pope was a saintly man and always open to whatever he sensed the Holy Spirit was prompting. Why not give him a call and have a frank talk with him and share what he would like to do? Dick was amazed at David's boldness but agreed it was probably the only course with any possible hope. All the others were dead ends. By midnight they agreed that David would call the Pope, discuss the matter with him, and take his chances.

Considering the time difference, they waited until after two o'clock in the morning before placing the call. The two men were like kids keyed up over an exciting new game, but they felt trepidation over the stakes involved. David had the Pope's private number. He was shocked to get him on the first try. *"Buon giorno, Giovanni parlando. Dio vi benedica."*

"Good morning, Holy Father, this is David Campbell."

Before David could say another word, the Pope broke in. "David, David, congratulations on your appointment. I was delighted when the prefect told me you had been selected. I can't tell you how happy I am for you. I know you will make a good bishop, though I suspect we are going to be talking quite a bit in the future. I know you like a son, and I have to admit I am a little apprehensive. I also know you didn't call this morning just to say hello. It must be the middle of the night where you are. How can I help you, David?"

"Holy Father, bear with me," David started. "I have an excellent priest here whom the whole diocese loves. I'll be brief. He wants to marry and insists on continuing as a priest. I can vouch that he has a vocation. I am reluctant to have him apply for a dispensation from celibacy, because the dispensation demands that he admit that he never had a vocation. That's dishonest and just not true. I know he won't go along with it and neither can I."

"David, calm down. I agree with you. I have felt for a long time the law is archaic. Celibacy is a beautiful virtue when it is free and a gift from God, but we can't demand God's gifts by papal mandate. The harshness of the law troubles me deeply, but I'm afraid of causing turmoil in conservative countries if I make changes. I agonize over this, David, more than you could imagine."

"I know, Holy Father. I remember our discussions of years ago. However, I have to live with myself now that you have made me bishop. I can't be party to a lie. I really want to help this priest, and I think we have to face the issue once and for all before we destroy our priesthood. There are obviously two gifts involved here: the call to the priesthood and the gift of celibacy. If the Holy Spirit gives a man the call to the priesthood but not the gift of celibacy, then we can destroy him by demanding something he has no grace from God to accomplish. We must be sensitive to how the Holy Spirit is working. This man clearly has a call to the priesthood, and just as clearly does not have the call to celibacy. Holy Father, as his bishop I feel I have to protect him and be obedient to the Holy Spirit."

"David, David, my son, you haven't changed one bit from your seminary days. That's why I always loved you so much. I knew we would one day find ourselves in this predicament. I also realize you won't give up on this, and I'm not going to be insistent, because in principle I agree with you. We should, however, follow the proper procedure. Have the priest apply for the dispensation. This is more for your benefit. I don't want you to get a reputation for ignoring procedures. I'll have someone here work on it with me and delete the ordinary requirements for the dispensation. Now, David, be patient on this and don't jump ahead. We'll go one step at a time."

"Thank you, Holy Father," David said. "You have settled my mind. At least there's hope we can finally approach this issue in a reasonable way."

"One last thing, David. Please stop calling me 'Holy Father.' I do have a name, you know. My name is John."

"Thank you, Holy Father," David said, embarrassed.

It was about three o'clock when David hung up. Dick had picked up the gist of the conversation and was thrilled it had gone so well. The two men hugged one another, laughing with delight. An impossible dream— and so far it was working.

Dick left David's house promising to do what he could to help Ed Marcel file his petition for the dispensation. He would wait on David's call before initiating the process. David warned Dick to keep the matter of the phone call to himself and not even share it with Ed. It could work to everyone's disadvantage if it leaked out the Pope was sidestepping established procedures.

6

ED HAD STOPPED off to visit Maureen after work and told her about his talk with the bishop. She listened but was skeptical, finding it hard to believe a bishop would stick his neck out to help.

"We can trust David," Ed insisted as he plopped down on the sofa next to Maureen.

"Ed, face it. They may be churchmen, but they are churchmen not because they are spiritual, but because it's their chosen field of politics. Even the best of them are political, and no politician is going to jeopardize his future for someone else's cause. I work with them all day long. David's no different, even though I like him. I'd be surprised if he'd make an issue of this and jeopardize himself just for you. The whole problem of celibacy could be resolved tomorrow if the bishops took a united stand against it. They are more concerned about their own positions than the long-term good of the Church. How can you expect one bishop to do what all of them united don't have the courage to do?"

"Maureen, you're too cynical," Ed said with a trace of annoyance. "I really am convinced David will fight for us. Give him a chance."

"That's one of your problems, Ed," Maureen countered. "You're too ready to see goodness in everyone. I'm just afraid you're going to be terribly hurt someday. Everyone isn't as unselfish as you are. As soon as people are threatened they cave in. Just watch. As I told you before, I have no trouble making a personal commitment to you before God and being content with you doing the same to me—we don't need a formal ceremony for that. Although it's not legal, I'm sure it wouldn't bother God. He's concerned with commitments, not legalities. This way you could still function as a priest and avoid the canonical trap of doing something that would incur their wrath. They are not unaware of real life. It's only when you make the commitment legal that they will punish you. So don't fall into their trap."

"Maureen, I have to be honest with myself. My love for you is deep enough to want to be open about our relationship and take my chances. I am willing to fight for my convictions. I feel the law is a gross violation of a human right—it's immoral. Church leaders fly in the face of the Holy Spirit, who has given a call to men like me who don't also have the gift of celibacy. A sensitive and caring hierarchy should be the first to respond to the way the Holy Spirit is working and not be so quick to punish. It is a shame decent people don't write and express their feelings to the Vatican. It's the people's Church, not the hierarchy's. Their only role is to be the servants of God's children, not their masters. They should be the first to interpret the Holy Spirit working in people's lives. One hundred twenty-five thousand good priests cut off from the sacraments makes a very powerful statement that something's wrong. They are not evil men, and they had vocations. If enough people wrote and demanded change, they'd change. They don't believe in democracy, but they believe that the Holy Spirit speaks through the united voice of the people throughout the Church." Ed finally stopped for a breath.

"Ed, maybe that's why I love you. You are such an incorrigible idealist, and so pure. You are a beautiful person," Maureen said as she leaned over and kissed him tenderly. Ed embraced her and kissed her in return, but with much more feeling.

David waited just a week before calling Ed Marcel. It had been a busy week, with the end of the school year and graduations of all sorts and the endless round of confirmations throughout the diocese. David asked if Ed still felt the same as he did the week before. The answer was definite. Could Ed come in to see David the next morning first thing? Ed would be there.

Ed arrived on schedule. After picking up coffee and donuts in the kitchen, the two men went into David's office. David left word with his secretary he was not to be disturbed.

"Ed, has anything changed since we last met?" David started.

"No, David, I still feel the same. If anything, more convinced than ever that this is something I must do," the priest responded.

"Just asking, Ed. I meant nothing by it. I've already talked to Dick Franey about your situation. In fact, we stayed up a whole night trying to work out something that might be viable. He is willing to work with you on it. This is our strategy: You apply for the dispensation from celibacy, then—"

"Wait a minute, David," Ed protested. "There's no way I'm going to apply for laicization. I've seen Tom Mahoney's papers. They're an insult to a priest's intelligence and an affront to one's priesthood. I'll be damned if I'll deny I have a call to the priesthood and admit my priesthood was a mistake. It wasn't a mistake. I refuse to deny that God has called me. They'll have to admit first that they put an obstacle in the way of my fulfilling my calling, but I know I have been called."

"Ed, calm down, or we're not going to get anywhere with this. I'm willing to help, but you have to be reasonable. You have to apply for the dispensation. That has to be the first step, or we will be in defiance of Church law, and that would become the issue and a serious obstacle to working this thing out. Trust me. I have worked out a deal, and those demands will not be in the dispensation."

"A deal with whom?" Ed asked immediately.

"That's not important. Just believe me," David answered.

"All right, but then what?" Ed asked impatiently.

"Then we'll have to discuss an assignment that will be discreet and at the same time not too inconvenient for you and Maureen. We can't just think in terms of yourself anymore."

"What kind of an assignment?" Ed asked warily.

"I don't know yet. It will be an assignment as a priest, don't worry, but I have to be as prudent as possible so as not to stir up a hornet's nest. Some priests will resent it. You'll be surprised how your own will give you the hardest time. The laypeople, God bless them, I know they'll go along with it."

"What's the next step?" Ed went on.

"The next step is for you to talk to Dick. He'll work with you on all the details. Then we'll move along one step at a time, carefully."

"How long is all this going to take?" Ed asked, concerned.

"Hopefully not more than a few months," David answered, trying to be reassuring.

"I have a hard time believing it, David, though I do trust you."

"It would be best for all of us if we keep the matter to ourselves. Any publicity beforehand could scuttle the plan before it sees the light of day," David said in warning.

"I understand, David, and I give you my word on it."

Ed thanked the bishop as the two men hugged, then David accompanied the priest to the door.

Back at his desk, David worked on a memo. The priest who refused to baptize Janet Maynard's baby a few weeks back was still on David's mind. Since then another incident had surfaced, and it was bothering him. This was something he could not allow any longer. He called in the chancellor and asked him to prepare a memo to all the priests in the diocese specifying that no priest was to refuse to baptize an infant unless both parents refused to raise the child as a Christian, or if the priest had solid evidence that not even one of the parents was willing to see to the Christian upbringing of the child. Nonattendance at Mass was not to be considered sufficient evidence, since there could be any number of reasons why parents might not attend church.

"Bishop, I think that's too lenient," the chancellor objected. "Many of these people never go to church, and the pastors feel they are being used."

"That may be true," David answered, "but many of these people have not had much instruction themselves, so their own faith may be weak. We should not be too quick to extinguish the smoldering wick. What we have to do is find ways to rekindle their faith. Being harsh and refusing to baptize a baby is only another example of the Church being judgmental and vindictive. You don't see that in the Good Shepherd. We all have to learn how to be good shepherds. I realize there is a problem, and I think the way it can be solved is by selecting parishioners to meet with parents of children to be baptized and prepare them for the ceremony, then continue to meet with them afterward to socialize and invite them to be part of activities with them. In this way the community shows it is interested in the people, and by caring draws them closer to Christ. That is the Christlike way of handling the problem. The other way is uncaring and short-sighted, and unfitting for a priest, and I don't think we should allow it in our diocese."

Charles didn't agree, and it was obvious though he said nothing. "I'll have the guidelines drawn up after lunch, David, and you can read them over. They should be ready to be sent out by tomorrow if that is all right."

"That will be fine, Charles. Thank you."

The chancellor went to his office seething. He had been encouraging the priests to take a hard line with people in the matter of baptism. To issue a memo to the contrary was distasteful, but he would swallow it . . . for the time being.

The afternoon was spent on ordinary business. David finished early and went home to work in his garden. It was a good time to plant onions, lettuce, and snap peas. He was determined to get an early start this year so he'd have a nice-looking garden by midsummer.

The drive from the city to his house on the outskirts of town was relaxing. David enjoyed driving by himself. It was peaceful and gave him a chance to think undisturbed. No people barging in to talk to him, no telephones, no distractions; it was the perfect time to think. That was when David did much of his heavy thinking, in fact, while driving to and from work each day.

It was an ideal day to work in the garden. The air was warm and the sun bright. The birds were singing cheerfully. David changed into his work clothes and went out into the garden. There was a big field to the left of David's house, which he let a farmer mow for hay. David worked the little piece of land on the other side of the house. The garden wasn't much more than a quarter acre in size, not terribly big but large enough for one man to work in his spare time.

No sooner had he started working than he was distracted by someone standing near the wall of his garden. It was Joshua again. This time David was excited to see him. He had so many questions to ask him.

"Joshua," he said with happy surprise in his voice, "I'm really glad you stopped by. I've been wanting to talk with you. Can you climb over that wall?"

The wall was only about four feet high, not much of a barrier for a man of Joshua's agility. David met him as he climbed over the wall, and the two men shook hands.

"Can I help you with your garden?" Joshua asked. "I like to help things grow."

"Yes, I'd appreciate that if you don't mind. I have a lot of things to ask you, and we can talk while we work."

David already had some rows neatly dug for the lettuce. They were perfectly straight. He asked Joshua if he would plant the lettuce.

"Yes. Is this it on the ground?" Joshua asked.

"Yes, that's it."

"Do you have some water to dip the roots in first?" Joshua asked.

"Over there," David said, directing him to a faucet sticking out of the ground at the side of the garden.

Joshua picked up a pail near the faucet and filled it with water then carried it back to where he was working.

"It sure is beautiful weather to work in the garden," David said as he carefully hoed the furrows for the next rows of lettuce.

"Yes, we're fortunate," Joshua replied as he kept working, soaking each tender lettuce plant in the water before he planted it.

"Joshua, you know, you have me wondering," David said.

"About what?"

"About your visit here a few weeks ago. It shocked me."

"Why?"

"Because I had seen you in a dream the night of my ordination. When I saw you walking down the street I couldn't believe it. I had thought you were just a fantasy, and to see you in real life was an eerie experience. The way you spoke to me made me feel as if you knew me."

"I do know you, David. I also know that God has chosen you for something very special," Joshua responded.

"What is that?" David asked, then quickly added, "and how do you know?"

"In time you will see the way God is working. I know because I can see clearly what He is accomplishing in your life. The world has to change. The Church must change if it is to be responsive to the needs of a rapidly changing world. Truths don't change, but there are different truths that have different meanings at different times in people's lives. A good shepherd will know how to carefully use the new and the old, like the wise scribe Jesus talked about, who knew how to take from his storehouse the new and the old and make them work together. You have a good chance to do that, David. The young priest is a good example. He has been called by God. It is also true that my Father does not intend for him to be alone. He needs a companion to love, and that is not demeaning or unclean. Love is beautiful. You are *his* shepherd also, David, and you must help him."

The young bishop almost dropped his hoe. How in God's name did this stranger know about Ed Marcel? As he looked at Joshua, the man just kept planting away as if nothing unusual had occurred.

"Joshua, how do you know about him?" David asked, bewildered.

"David, don't ask so many questions. I will help you when you need me, but ask me what you need to know, and we will leave the rest for another time." Joshua looked up at David with a broad smile. David relaxed, but he was still bewildered, even though he also felt a strange peace, like the peace he felt when he saw Joshua for the first time, in the dream.

"So you think I'm on the right track with that priest, Joshua?" David asked.

"David, there is no other way. Love is a right God has given to His children. No one has authority to deny a right that God has given. To work alone for the kingdom is desirable at times, and sometimes necessary, but it has to be a free choice, not a mandate. It is insensitive and offensive to God to deny a person the right to follow God's call because he chooses to love honestly. It is doing irreparable harm to the Church and drawing the wrong people into the vineyard."

Joshua remained on his knees while talking, looking up occasionally at David, who was leaning on his hoe listening attentively.

"You had better keep hoeing, David, or I'm not going to have any place for these plants," Joshua reminded his friend.

"Sorry. What you just said makes sense, and it is the way I feel about it. However, I don't know how successful I'm going to be in helping this fellow," David remarked.

"At least you are making a start," Joshua responded. "You have the support you need in the right place, and that assures you of success. Just do what you know you should do. The rest is God's business."

David was wondering if Joshua knew about the Pope's involvement but didn't dare ask.

After that exchange the two men continued working, saying little. When they finished, David invited Joshua to stay for supper. He politely declined but said he would be glad to accept on another occasion. Joshua left and David went into the house, his mind alive with excitement as he washed and prepared for supper.

7

"**J**OAN, would you call Father O'Donnell out in the valley and ask if tonight is a good night for me to come out for supper?" David said to his corresponding secretary. That was the first order of business for the day. David was impatient to get started on his program to revitalize the communities throughout the diocese.

In a few minutes she called back to say that tonight would be fine, and said the priest wanted to know what he would like for supper. David told her and said he should be expected at the rectory at around five-thirty.

After that he went over various papers and memos the staff had left on his desk. Among them was the memo to the priests setting guidelines for baptism. Considering his attitude on the matter, Charles had done a good job interpreting the bishop's mind on the subject, so David accepted the document with only a few minor suggestions and called the chancellor to tell him to issue it.

While discussing the memo, David also asked Charles how far along he was on the matter of transferring diocesan agencies to lay control. The chancellor had met with various department heads and asked for their suggestions, he informed David. Some thought it was a good idea and had practical recommendations as to how to implement the proposal; others were quite negative. David could sense Charles's reluctance to go through with the plan, so he asked him to bring in whatever notes he had on the matter and the two of them would go over it together.

The social services agency of the diocese was David's big concern. David was determined that the major thrust of the charitable work of the churches had to be at the local level. To put costly institutions in the seat of the diocese, while impressive, would drain diocesan resources and deny people in the farther reaches of the diocese aid that was absolutely necessary.

"Charles, tonight I am going out to the valley to have dinner with Bill O'Donnell. I'd like to share with him my reorganization plan and see how he feels about it. His place is so far removed from everyone his people have practically no chance to share in the resources of the diocese. Bill has a lot of common sense, and he should have some practical suggestions as to how we can implement this idea."

The chancellor said nothing. David could tell he was not the slightest bit interested in the proposal and had hoped David would have forgotten about it.

"What do you intend to do with the director and the staff? Are you just going to fire them?" Charles asked bluntly, showing very clearly his disdain for the whole idea.

"Not at all, Charles. The operation can still be directed from a central office, but I don't see any need for the clergy's involvement. There's no reason why the laypeople cannot run the program and make all the decisions. They will have to work out the details for the financing, but if they do their work well the people will support them. They may have to cut back on some programs here in the city so they can reach out to the local communities. I feel the people will be so happy to see the diocese's presence in their areas that they will be most supportive."

"Well, I hope so, David," was all Charles could say.

David was having a problem with Charles's attitude. He felt he should get rid of him immediately and appoint someone more supportive, someone who would be, if only from a human point of view, more fun, but he was trying hard to be a good shepherd like Jesus, who Himself had difficulties with the apostles who could be so dense and so crude.

"Well, Charles, I think we are at least off to a good start. I would like you to contact the director of the charities and have him come in so I can discuss the changes with him, and the sooner the better. I want to get this thing started before I get bogged down with other things. I can see how one can get overwhelmed around here."

"I'll get to it today, and we should be able to get things going in a day or two," Charles said as he was getting up to leave.

"One more thing, Charles." David suddenly remembered something. "I would like you to set a date for a clergy conference. I want to speak to all the priests and deacons. Invite the deacons' wives, too."

"When would you like to have it, Bishop?" Charles

asked, betraying his detached attitude by slipping into a formal address.

"In three weeks if it is not too short a notice."

The chancery staff was beginning to feel more comfortable with David as each day passed. He was so relaxed, so casual. It was not a put-on casualness, with an underlying tenseness that made everyone feel uneasy, but a genuinely relaxed manner that put people at ease. He was always ready to crack a joke or laugh at someone else's humor. People found themselves looking forward to lunch if they knew David was going to be there. Even the few who had been going out for lunch were now eating with the others. It was fast becoming a close-knit family.

David stopped off at his own house a little later in the afternoon to take a rest before going out to the valley. It had been a strenuous day already, and he knew he would be coming home late. Besides, he always enjoyed supper more after a good rest.

It was exactly five-thirty when David arrived at Bill O'Donnell's place. The drive out was invigorating. The air was light; the smell of fresh manure in the fields was a strong reminder that summer was fast approaching. Daffodils and tulips were springing up in just about everyone's yard and in fields along the way. David always enjoyed driving through the country in this kind of weather, especially at this time of the year.

The housekeeper answered the door immediately, as if she had been standing there waiting, and became flustered when the bishop introduced himself.

"I am David Campbell. I think Father O'Donnell is expecting me."

"Oh, yes, Bishop. He is expecting you. He should be down in a minute. My name is Bridie O'Shaughnessy. I'm the cook and housekeeper here."

She had never welcomed a bishop before but managed to keep her composure even though she was all aflutter inside.

"Bishop, would you come with me," she said as she escorted him to the living room.

The room was a large room well appointed with gorgeous contemporary furniture.

"Bishop, would you sit down and make yourself at home? I'll tell Father you're here."

David picked up a magazine lying on the coffee table and sat down while the housekeeper scrambled to announce his arrival. The pastor was already on his way down the stairs when he encountered the housekeeper. Entering the living room, he warmly welcomed his guest.

"Bishop, I'm honored that you should come all the way out here to visit me. I've never had a bishop visit me before."

David stood up when the priest entered. "I intend to visit all the priests if I can, Bill. You are precious to me. I exist for you. Priests don't exist for their bishop, and I would like the priests to know that I want to be of service to them, and not the other way around."

The priest was shocked to hear such a thing coming from a bishop. In the past, priests *did* exist just to do the bishop's bidding and to support whatever programs the bishop saw fit to institute. From one point of view they were the chief money raisers for the bishop's projects and were often assigned accordingly. Priests knew that and so set their priorities.

"Bishop, would you like to come upstairs and relax, or do you feel comfortable enough in the living room?" the pastor asked, feeling a little unsure of how best to entertain a bishop.

"This is fine, Bill, and please call me David. I want to be your friend as well as your bishop. That's important to me."

"Thank you, David. You honor me in saying that. Bridie made some hors d'oeuvres. Would you like a cocktail before we settle down for dinner? I have just about everything."

"How about a Southern Comfort old-fashioned, with no water?"

"You don't fool around, do you?"

"I don't drink much, but I like my drinks strong," David replied.

Although at his own house David never talked business before or during supper, when visiting he followed his host's custom, and Bill O'Donnell couldn't wait to ply David with a thousand questions—albeit discreetly.

David answered them and used each to share bits of information he wanted circulated. He was a master at insinuating things he wanted people to talk about. It was his way of keeping people's attention on things he felt were important.

"Bill, you are at the farthest limits of the diocese. How do you see the diocese helping you to do things you feel are important for your people and for your community? And I don't mean just Catholics."

"Wow, that's some question, David. I don't know whether I am prepared to answer it," Bill responded, taken aback.

"Try, and take your time."

"Well, our area is poor. As you can tell by looking at our financial reports, we have a hard time making ends meet. One of the most difficult problems for people out here is their inability to get emergency medical care. The hospitals are so far away. Many of the people do not have medical insurance, and some have been turned away from the hospital because they couldn't pay."

"What do you think would be needed to alleviate that problem?" David asked, concerned.

"I really don't know. I've never thought too much about it," the pastor replied.

"Do you think you could get the community to work together and plan for a clinic if we were to give you some help financially?"

"What do you mean by 'community'? You mean our own people?" the pastor asked.

"No, everyone, the Protestant people, the ministers, the rabbi, and key laypeople from the community at large. You see, Bill, I feel my role as bishop is to be of service to all the priests and people. You are the ones who are on the firing line faced with all the dire needs of the people. I want to help."

The pastor couldn't believe his ears. No bishop had ever spoken to him like that before. It was difficult for this simple pastor to imagine the bishop could even be interested in the problems of his parish, much less his community, and what is more, care enough to want to do something about it. Tears began to well up in the priest's eyes.

"David, forgive me. I'm just overwhelmed. You can't imagine how alone and forgotten I've felt out here. I thought no one ever cared what I did, or whether I even existed, and for you to offer to help me with my work here, I, well, it's just too much to comprehend."

"I do mean it, Bill. I want to help. If you could use a clinic, I would be willing to share some of the money from the diocesan funds to help you get started. I feel strongly that the needs are out here, in places like this, and our resources should be spread around rather than just concentrated on the big cities."

"David, I agree. You don't know how demoralizing it is to see all the money going to places where our people will never benefit. I am deeply touched by your gesture, and I'm sure our people will be, too. Even though they don't have much, they will be more generous than ever in giving of themselves."

"In looking at the map," David said, "I noticed that there is a good number of well-populated villages in the area. If you could get everyone to work together, there may be other things we might do to develop a functioning Christian community that would include not just our own but others who are concerned. I would like to see that as our goal, Bill. Do you think it is something we can work toward? With the dwindling number of priests, it is essential that we stay in the background and let the people assume as much of the leadership as possible."

"David, I would be more than delighted to do what

I can. The people will be ecstatic when I tell them," the priest said, filling up with emotion.

After a feast of such sharing of dreams, the meal was anticlimactic. Bridie did a good job of cooking, and David made her feel as if he had never tasted anything like it. After supper, the two men had a cordial and a cup of coffee, then David left for home.

Father O'Donnell couldn't wait for the night to end so he could tell everyone about the bishop's visit, starting with his fellow priests, then his Protestant clergy friends, and, finally, his key laypeople. He had just become the best public relations man that David could have. Each of the priests he told hoped he would be next on the bishop's dinner circuit.

The rest of the week went by in a flash. David had accomplished a lot that week and was looking forward to Sunday. He had important things to say in his weekly sermon. The news team no longer came to the cathedral out of necessity, but each pronouncement from David was a news event in itself, which the reporters enjoyed and even looked forward to hearing.

The cathedral Mass that Sunday was packed. Attendance had been gradually increasing each week, with the crowd growing as the word spread. This Sunday was by far the best attended yet, and it made David feel as if his people were responding to what he had to say. His sermon this Sunday was about a topic that troubled him all during his life as a priest, namely, the many people who questioned the existence of God.

"My dear people," David began his sermon, "I have had a good week and at times a bit of a terrifying week.

I had a chance during the course of the week to see how some of our people are hurting. I also came across a man who did not believe in God. I have met people like this before, but this man impressed me. He wasn't angry or cynical, or even antagonistic. He was very calm and matter-of-fact about his atheism. That is what troubled me. I met him at a gas station. He was pumping gas for an old lady who had pulled into the station just before he did. I was impressed. I struck up a conversation with him. He asked if I wasn't the new bishop. I told him yes, and I asked him if I had seen him in church. 'Not likely, Bishop. I don't believe in God.'

" 'Why?' I asked him. He answered very matter-of-factly that every morning he woke up and found everything right here, the whole world and everything in it. Why could it not have been that way from the beginning? He was sure people a million years ago had the same thought when they woke up in the morning. Everything was always there. Why could it not have always been that way? Why do we need any further explanation than that the world and the universe were always here? When people say there's a God, and you ask them where He came from, they will say He was always there. Why could not the same be said of the universe, it was always here?

"I had never heard it put quite that way before and I could see how a person could slip into that way of thinking. The man also added that he had seen a lot of hurt in his lifetime and could not imagine a caring God allowing all that misery.

"It was hard for me to take exception to what he said, because, frankly, I myself sometimes have diffi-

culty understanding why God allows so much hurt and
pain.

"I was at a loss for the moment as to how to respond.
I felt I wanted to say something, but it was only after he
left that a thought occurred to me, which I'd like to
share with you. If you were blind and you felt a strong
heat warming the front of your body, you would know
that there was a heat source somewhere in front of you.
If you smelled a sweet fragrance floating all around you,
you would know by instinct there was something that
exuded that pleasant-smelling perfume. If you heard the
most enchanting music would you not also conclude that
there were people responsible for such beautifully arranged notes? With all the beautiful objects and events
that fill our world, it takes more faith to believe they
resulted from a series of accidents than to believe there
was some intelligent Goodness responsible for them.
And if that Goodness gave us a superabundance of resources and said 'Share with one another' and we did
not, so that many were left deprived and hurting, could
He be blamed for all the resulting misery?

"There is enough genius and food and natural resources to resolve most of the world's problems, but so
often we don't care, and we are content to make sure our
own needs and those of our family are met. We should
learn to feel responsible for other of God's children that
He places in our paths. Each of us must learn to be the
hands and lips and heart of Christ, bringing His healing
love into a world that hurts so much and sharing with
those who have little the gifts He has loaned so gener-
ously to us. By channeling God's gifts to a hurting world,
we become the strongest proof that God exists."

That was the gist of David's talk. It was typical of the simple but touching way he spoke to the people. It revealed the clarity and depth of his own perception of the most profound ideas, and he spoke in an uncritical but caring way, much the way Jesus once did.

When David had got to the middle of his sermon he noticed to his surprise Joshua sitting in the back pew, looking up at him and listening attentively. Now, thinking he would see him afterward, he was disappointed that he was nowhere in sight.

THE DAY for the clergy conference arrived. The priests, deacons, and their wives all came. It was the first time some of the priests had met David, so it was more a get-acquainted party than a conference to iron out problems. David did, however, have some things he wanted to discuss with the priests. One of the most important was his direction for the near future. He took no time in getting right to the point.

"Ladies and gentlemen," he started, "I am most grateful to all of you for the support and kindness you have shown me since my ordination. I am fortunate to have such an unusually fine group of men and women to work with. Having worked among you myself for so many years, I understand some of the burdens and pressures under which you all labor. It is not easy. I also realize that it is possible to sometimes feel that you exist just to provide support for the things I am interested in and to raise funds for the diocese, which occupies almost one fourth of the year timewise. I want to assure you that you are not money raisers, and I do not intend that you be pressured to do this kind of work in the future. You haven't been ordained for that. Nor have you been ordained to support the bishop's pet projects. You have been ordained to provide leadership to the Christian communities you have been assigned to and to preach the word of God in season and out of season. It is my role to support you in this. So I intend to visit each of your communities in time and become more intimately acquainted with all of you and your people, and to provide you with the support you need to guide your people. I fully intend to be at your service when you need me. I see that as my chief role as bishop, to provide you with the guidance and support you need to extend the kingdom of God.

"One of the problems facing the Church today is the critical need to respond to people's desperate search for a religion that makes sense, and to hear the word of God preached to them by their priests. People hunger for spirituality. They are tired of packaged religion. They crave God and an intimacy with God. It is difficult to provide this in a ten-minute sermon on a Saturday afternoon or a Sunday morning. There are also so many people today who have never heard of Christ and know nothing about His message. Locked in our parishes, resaving the same souls day after day, paralyzes your ability to bring the word of God to a world that needs the message of Jesus more than ever before. It is essential that you be free to do precisely that, to bring the message of Jesus to all the unchurched people in the communities around you. Our people today are well educated. They run their businesses and their local governments and their various community projects with efficiency and expertise. There is no reason why they can't administer with love and sensitivity their own Christian communities, taking the focus of the parishes off the buildings themselves and refocusing their attention where it should be properly placed—on the people, their needs, their dreams, their aspirations for their church. With your own new freedom, you will still provide direction and spiritual leadership to your parishes, but you will also be free to bring the message of Christ outside your parish and into the community at large, not by evangelizing other Christians, which would be cynical and regressive, but by bringing a real living Jesus to the many people who do not yet know Him.

"I won't share with you today all the details of this dream, but I would like you to just think about it until we can find our way to implement it. Suffice it to say that we will be trying a few experiments in this area to test the waters and garner some valuable experience before we expand it throughout the diocese. I do hope you will be patient with me as I grope along in areas in which I have no experience and no expertise. I can honestly say I never really practiced being bishop, so it's all very new to me. I desperately need your prayers, your understanding, and your patience.

"Another issue that deeply troubles me is the role of women in the Church. They should be allowed to play a much more vital official function. I intend to do what I can to bring that about in our own diocese and at bishops' conferences."

After these comments David shared with the priests his plans for the schools throughout the diocese. That caught them all off guard. Opinions afterward were varied, some favorable, some critical, and some downright hostile.

Though David seemingly worked in low gear, things were happening on many fronts, and in rapid succession. The social service director had met with David, and although his apprehension was obvious, he was happy to cooperate with his new bishop, as much from fear of losing his job as from a willingness to be helpful. He did not agree with the plan; it appeared to be dismantling a good thing, a well-established bureaucracy that gave him high public profile and status among his official state counterparts. David, however, was determined to make his ministry effective in touching as many lives as possible.

Father Ed Marcel's petition for dispensation had been filed. Father Bill O'Donnell could not wait to spread the news about the bishop's proposal for the area and the plans for the clinic. David had also met with executives from several large corporations to test their feelings about a cooperative role in the managing of the diocesan schools. There were thirty-five elementary schools and nine high schools in the diocese. They were relatively well run, and the buildings were in good condition, most having been built within the past thirty years. Not filled to capacity, they could still handle considerably more students, a positive factor because it gave David a chance to expand the operation and open the school to children of other religions. He wanted to make them truly ecumenical schools where children of all religions could receive excellent training, not just in academics, technical, and artistic subjects, but in solid religious values as well. Since people of different religions lived and worked side by side it was important that the school environment be open to all young people so they could learn to live together and appreciate each other's varied experiences.

As to how David planned to staff the school and provide for all the new courses would become the chief concern of the businesspeople. David's idea was simple: with personnel from their companies, of course. Industry had perennially benefited from the training and education of its employees at taxpayers' expenses, so why not assign some of these highly educated people to teach in the schools? They had artists, electronic experts, designers, printers, computer scientists, a vast reservoir of talent already working in their fields, who could be an inspiration to the students if they spent some time in the classroom.

Before long, the businesspeople were warming up to the bishop's dream. They began to see how the program could benefit their companies. After all, these schools would act as economical apprenticeship schools for industries. They also understood and appreciated David's concern that they continue to instill spiritual values in the students. Yes, there definitely was potential to the proposal, and they would be glad to bring back the idea to their people for further consideration.

David's life was fast being caught up in a maelstrom of activity. The chancery staff could not believe what was happening; David seemed so easygoing and so calm about everything. Most of the staff was positive and enjoyed being part of what was happening, but Charles Mayberry was more unhappy than ever seeing the bishop successful in his radical dreams. His phone calls to the archbishop were almost daily now, and the archbishop himself was becoming more concerned about David's long-term goals. The archbishop was extremely traditional and prided himself on being the watchdog of orthodoxy and the guardian of tradition. The new bishop was proving to be a maverick who cared little for the way things had been done in the past, and it seemed he could go off in any direction and throw the whole Church into confusion. The effects of one bishop straying from the path of rigid uniformity could be catastrophic in its repercussions on every other diocese in the country. If his ideas took hold, other bishops would be pressured to follow suit, and the ensuing trend would put uneasy pressure on the Vatican to react.

It was early Monday morning when David received a phone call from the archbishop.

"Hello, David, this is Archbishop O'Connell."

"Hello, Bishop," David replied, "how kind of you to call."

The archbishop was in no mood to be sociable. He had something on his mind. "David, I have been receiving complaints about some things you are doing in your diocese, and I would like you to come down here so we can discuss them."

"Could you tell me what they might be so I could have some idea what these dreadful rumors are all about?" David queried.

"I would rather not discuss them over the phone. Could you come here within the next few days so we can talk them over?" the archbishop continued.

David was in an uncomfortable position. As a bishop he was autonomous in his own diocese, and even though the archbishop was the metropolitan, he had no legal jurisdiction over David's diocese. For David to comply

with the archbishop's instructions to come for an obvious dressing down was demeaning. It was important to
preserve his integrity as a bishop if he was to be effective
in bringing about the change he judged essential to the
good of the Church.

"Really, Bishop," David responded as gently as he
could, "I am at a loss as to what there is to discuss.
These are matters that are internal to my diocese, and I
can't see how they could be troubling anyone else."

"David, maybe you don't understand how we work.
No bishop is a law unto himself, and no diocese is an
island. Everything a bishop does affects every other
bishop, and the Church everywhere. Solidarity among
bishops is a necessity if the Church is to survive."

David was determined to hold his line. "Solidarity
is one thing, Bishop," David replied, "but rigid conformity merely shackles the Church and prevents the
honest facing of problems, paralyzing any attempt to
resolve the most critical of issues. If we operate that
way the Church is doomed. Token response to people's
needs is more frustrating than no help at all, because
it holds out the false hope that we are willing to
change when we are not. What I have done, Bishop, is
nothing more than any reasonable, caring bishop
should do."

"David," the archbishop interjected with thinly dis-
guised impatience, "I insist we discuss the matter."

David's initial impulse was intense anger. He sup-
pressed it only with the greatest difficulty. "Bishop," he
said in a gentle voice that carefully masked his true
feelings, "I have a full schedule that would make it
impossible for me to take the whole day off. If we could

meet halfway, I think it could be arranged. Perhaps we could meet at L'Ecole for lunch or early dinner."

The archbishop was furious at being treated in such an offhanded manner, but at least David's suggestion was not an outright refusal, and he was constrained to accept if he really wanted to discuss what was bothering him. "Very well, David, I'll meet with you halfway, at L'Ecole. My secretary will work out the details with your secretary," the archbishop ended by saying, thus assuming the last bit of control that was left to him. Both men hung up, neither very happy over the encounter.

Knowing that Charles was the cause of all this trouble with the archbishop, David was sorely tempted to fire him and ship him out to the farthest post in the diocese as a punishment for his treachery. David could be vengeful, though he was now trying to discipline this trait in his personality and do the Christlike thing. Jesus had his Judas, too. He knew Judas was unstable and would one day betray Him, but He let him remain with His band of followers right up to the end.

Self-preservation and high idealism were struggling within David, and there was no way he could come to a quick decision on this one. What troubled David about Charles was the sad fact that Charles was convinced he was doing God a favor by protecting tradition and preserving the sacred way the Church had always done things.

It bothered Charles that the old ways were being scuttled and that everything he had been taught was sacred was now being discarded as irrelevant. Latin had been the language of God, now it was no more. The old vestments and the old rites had been sacred; they too were no more. Protestants were once excommunicated and cut off from God; now they were being embraced as if they were right after all! Now this amateur bishop was dismantling the very role and function of bishop as he had always known it, radically changing the whole structure of the Christian community. It was too much.

Charles was God's defense against this sacrilege. He could see nothing good in his bishop. To his way of thinking David was the enemy—he was evil. Whatever Charles had to do was justified. Slander, libel, destroying the bishop's reputation would not be treachery; under these circumstances they would be virtues.

David knew this was the twisted logic that was driving Charles, and there was no way he could change the way Charles thought. It was impossible the two men would ever be able to work together harmoniously. But David was unable to resolve the issue right now. He dismissed it from his mind for the time being.

As luck would have it, practically every time David left his office that day he kept bumping into the chancellor. Charles could not look David in the eye. The encounters were tense. David tried to be pleasant. Charles found it increasingly difficult to be even civil. That he stayed on the job was a testament to his deep belief in his mission to undo David, have him deposed, do whatever else it took to rid the Church of this menace. Charles knew that David knew, and David's being so kind to him was like pouring salt into his wounds. This kindness and forgiveness that David was manifesting certainly did not fit with the image Charles had of David. Charles would have been more comfortable if David had been hostile.

The conversation with the archbishop cast a pall over the rest of David's day. That it should happen so early in his new position when he had spent his life avoiding tactical errors like this was humiliating. While he knew this would just be the beginning, however, David had no intention of turning back.

After a rather uneventful afternoon, David left for home. On the way he saw an elderly man walking along the highway. Ordinarily, David did not pick up hitchhikers, but the man seemed too dignified to be hitchhiking. He was neatly dressed and well groomed.

David stopped and yelled through the open window, "Would you like a lift, mister?"

"I sure would," was the reply.

"Where are you headed?"

"Coatesville, Pennsylvania. It's near Philly."

"What are you doing way up here?"

"Going from shelter to shelter. You can stay only a few nights in these places, then they make you leave."

"Somehow you don't look like the type who would be living in shelters. You seem to be a working man."

"I used to. Worked for the railroad for years until I retired. Been over ten years now and my pension isn't worth a damn. Right now I'm on my way back home to pick up my social security check at the post office."

"You have a home there?" David asked.

"Not anymore. Can't afford one. Can't even afford an apartment. I have to choose between food or rent. Can't afford both. I try to get little jobs here and there, but who wants to hire old men? Quite a few of my old friends are in the same boat. I bump into them occasionally. One day I found a dear friend who used to work with me lying on a park bench. I didn't recognize him at first, but then he called my name. He had been a switchman, one of the hardest-working men in my crew. His family had all died. He couldn't afford to pay the taxes on his house, so it went up for tax sale. Like myself he couldn't afford rent either, so he just wandered the streets looking for a place to sleep at night. When I found him that day he was in bad shape. I tried to get him some help, but he was too far gone. By the time someone came he was dead. Died in my arms. I cried like a baby. He had been one of my best friends during all those years on the railroad. Saved my life one day when I got my foot trapped in an automatic switching track. Poor Jake. He deserved a better end than that.

"I made arrangements for his funeral. The minister was kind. Wouldn't accept anything. I made a pine box myself since I couldn't afford one. There was no one at the funeral parlor anyway. We buried him in a pauper's plot. I prayed for him, though I'm sure he's with God. God always takes care of abandoned people like ourselves. I felt so alone when we lowered that coffin in the grave. I was sad for a week. Knew it would probably be my fate someday soon. I was lucky to survive this past winter. It was bitter cold, and I'm not used to living this way. If I drank, I suppose I could have deadened the pain, but I never drank in my life. What's happening today is a sad commentary on this land of opportunity.

"I saw a TV program recently where an outspoken moderator and another fellow from some university were ridiculing the homeless, saying we were good-for-nothing and bums and were in the streets only because we choose to be there. Insensitive, ignorant people if I ever saw them. If they only knew! Maybe they don't want to know. It would make them too uncomfortable, I guess. I think they're the kind of people Jesus talked about when He told the story of the rich man and the poor, starving leper."

Tears were trickling down David's cheeks as the old man told his story. He asked the man if he would like to come and stay with him. He could do some work around the house and help the gardener with the grounds during the summertime. The man was overjoyed.

"I still have to go down and get my check and whatever mail is waiting for me. Then I'll come back. Thank you so much. What are you, a minister or a priest?"

"Yes, I'm a priest. David Campbell is my name. Here's my card so you can get in touch with me. What's your name?"

"Bill Reinhardt, Father. I'm a tough ol' German."

David had already driven far out of his way to bring the man within striking distance of a truck stop where he would have a good chance to get a ride. As soon as he stopped to drop him off, a trucker was just leaving the yard. He recognized David.

"Hi, Bishop! Where's the gent going?"

"Near Philly, Don. Can you help us out?" David yelled back.

"Same direction I'm going. Hop in, ol'-timer. I'll take you the whole way."

The old man shook David's hand and, when he took his hand away, found in it a fifty-dollar bill. The man's eyes watered at the generosity of this stranger. He thanked him and got into the truck.

David finally arrived home, much later than he

planned. Changing his clothes, he went out into the garden to loosen the soil and set a few more plants. Since the weather was so pleasant he decided to develop another section of the garden and so broke up another piece of ground, arranged the rows, and started planting.

He had been working for only a few minutes when that friendly stranger, Joshua, passed by and shouted his greeting to David. David was genuinely glad to see Joshua. For some reason he was the only person David could open up to and share his deepest concerns.

"Hi, Joshua, I sure am glad to see you," David called out as the visitor walked across the lawn to the garden.

"Hello, David," Joshua replied. "Life can get complicated, can't it?"

David had come to accept Joshua's uncanny awareness of the details of his private life, so he simply responded, "It sure can. I never dreamed I would encounter the things that have been happening lately, and the trouble starts right in my own house. I know Jesus had a Judas. I have one, too, and I don't know how to handle it. I would like to fire him, but I don't think it would be the Christlike thing to do."

Casually picking up the hoe to help David in the garden, Joshua remarked, "Yes, that can be a difficult situation. Jesus did have that problem as He watched Judas shifting from loyalty to distrust and wavering more and more as the days passed. He thought many times of sending him off, but realized that he had a part to play in His Father's plan, so He decided to allow His Father to decide what to do with Judas."

"Sometimes I think that way," David mused, "but

then I resent what is happening and feel I have a right to protect myself."

"Yes, you do have that right," Joshua agreed, "but you also feel a need to allow God the freedom to execute His own plans for your life, and that is what confuses you, isn't it?"

"Yes," David said, laughing. "How do you know how I feel?"

Joshua let the question pass. "In trying to follow Jesus, you are doing an admirable thing, and my Father will not disappoint you. You need great faith to live that way, but if you can continue, the Father's plan will unfold in a way that will surprise you. God's love is so tender that He watches people's slightest steps and is always nearby to bring good out of even hurtful circumstances."

"Joshua, the problems I have with my chancellor are nothing compared to what is unfolding. I got a call from the archbishop this morning. He apparently does not approve of the way I am doing things and wants to see me for a dressing down. What troubles me is not that he's concerned, but it was his tone and manner. He didn't treat me as a brother or a colleague but as an inferior. We are both bishops, and each bishop has to have the freedom to work out the problems in his own diocese."

"You are right, David. Jesus established twelve apostles and gave them authority to teach and guide their flocks. Peter was special, but his authority is exercised best when it is done discreetly, as the need arises, and not in the everyday running of every other bishop's flock.

That undermines the integrity and authority Jesus gave to each apostle. Bishops should work together humbly and with due courtesy to one another, not lording it over others they deem less important. There is no room for this kind of authority in Jesus' family."

"I needed to hear that," David said to Joshua. "The archbishop is a good man, and I personally admire him in many ways, but he loves the first place at assemblies and demands a special throne when he meets publicly with other bishops. That mentality betrays a shallowness that ill befits a shepherd of God's people."

"Jesus noticed that same trait in the Scribes and Pharisees," Joshua said. "They loved the first places at public gatherings and special marks of reverence. It is sad that these people work their way up in the Church. They intimidate not only the sheep but the shepherds as well. Still, there are some in very high places who are beautiful people and treat their fellow bishops with sensitivity."

"Joshua," David said, "it is strange how freely I can talk to you about things I could never discuss with anyone. What is there about you that draws out of me all these hidden concerns? I guess it is because somehow I know you understand and are concerned. Maybe deep down I sense in some way you have come from God and you were sent to help me."

"David, to my Father everyone is special and each has a special work. You are special, and the work my Father has planned for you is very important. He has prepared you well. Indeed, your whole life up until now has been a careful preparation for the work my Father has planned for you. Because of this He is guiding your every step. You must not be afraid to follow where He leads."

"Joshua," David replied, "you talk about God as your father in the same say Jesus referred to Him. I would love to ask you a personal question, but I'm afraid it would be rude. I'll resist, though I would love to know more about you."

"David," Joshua answered gently, "in your heart you know who speaks to you and guides your life. You need know no more. Be content to trust God who guides your every step. He will always be by your side."

The two men had stopped working and were standing in the garden facing each other, David leaning on his hoe and Joshua holding a trowel. David was shocked to realize it was already suppertime.

"Joshua, look at the time," David remarked. "It is time to eat. Would you have supper with me? I'm not a bad cook, and I would enjoy talking to you further."

"I am hungry," Joshua acknowledged, "and would enjoy having supper with you."

With that the two men put their tools away, knocked the dirt from their shoes and sandals, and disappeared into the house.

It did not take David long to prepare supper. While it was cooking he placed a plate of cheese and crackers, chunks of cold cuts, and a bottle of wine on the coffee table in the den, where they retired for the next few minutes.

But it was too beautiful an evening to eat inside. David decided to bring everything out on the patio. Breaking his own rule of never talking business during meals, he plied Joshua with a thousand questions. One in particular brought a surprising response. What did Joshua think of all the Christian churches?

"I see you all as one family that has never learned to get along and whose members do not know how to treat one another. Each group thinks they are the only ones who are pleasing to God. That is sad because my Father sees all of you as flawed in so many ways, yet He still loves you. All you see is the blemish in each other and fail to see the blindness in yourselves. The Holy Spirit works through all of you. You think He works only through your own. You cannot reduce God to something so petty. You are all His children. The greatest sin is the failure to take steps to draw closer to one another, and your failure to imitate the Father in His love. That not only harms yourselves, but causes great scandal to the world around you, which should look to the Church for guidance and direction. That brokenness has to be healed if you are to be the light Jesus intended you to be. Your Church is the trunk. It is the rock. Peter is still the guide, but his role in the modern world is to steer the ship through troubled waters, while allowing the other shepherds the freedom to fulfill their responsibilities according to their own judgment. That is necessary if Peter is to be trusted by other shepherds. Jesus created twelve apostles, not one. When he assumes the role Jesus intended then there will easily be one flock."

David listened intently to Joshua's discourse, taking note of his mannerisms and his expressions as he spoke. He gestured with graceful movements; his face expressed changing emotions with such ease. His voice was soft and gentle, but it betrayed force in its deep conviction. David was amazed as he watched this beautiful man speak about sublime matters with such casualness.

Time went by quickly after supper. The two men talked far into the night, not noticing how late it had become. David apologized for keeping Joshua so late and insisted he stay for the evening. It was definitely too late to send him out into the streets. Joshua gently protested at first, then when David insisted, he agreed to stay.

David showed him to his room upstairs. It was a good-size room, with a striking painting of Jesus on the wall facing the door that caught one's eye on entering. An ethereal Jesus covered with a blue and white prayer shawl, hovering against the Weeping Wall with two Hasidic Jews facing the wall as they prayed. Jesus is looking down on them tenderly and with deep compassion, as he rests a hand on the shoulder of the man close to him.

Alone in his room, Joshua spent the good part of an hour absorbed in prayer before retiring.

The next morning, a visitor arrived just as David and Joshua were coming downstairs for breakfast. It was David's secretary, Father Jim Mohr, bringing a package of express mail that had been delivered after David left the chancery the day before. He thought it might be important and that the bishop might want to see it before coming to work. David invited him to stay for Mass and breakfast. The three of them sat down as David presided at the Breaking of Bread. At homily time, the three men shared thoughts. The subject of various Christians' understanding of the Eucharist was discussed, and how so many good people have been excluded from partaking of the Eucharist because of faulty faith or less than perfect lives. David wondered out loud what Jesus would do if certain Christians had gathered together in his presence for the Breaking of Bread.

Joshua's answer was simple and surprising. "At the Last Supper the apostles were far from perfect. They loved Jesus but still did not understand who He really was. Their faith at the time was very imperfect, and their holiness left much to be desired—in a few minutes they were all to abandon Him and deny even knowing Him. Jesus realized how imperfect they were but also knew their love for Him was genuine nonetheless, so He shared His flesh and blood with them."

CHAPTER

9

THE MEETING with the archbishop was cordial. The archbishop was a good man in spite of his rigid legalism, though he was pompous at times, and conservative, especially about customs, rules, pious religious practices—all those areas that David felt must change if the Church were to be relevant to a modern world. David himself had been conservative all his life, but his spiritual journey led him to see a distinction between what was essential to faith and the teachings of Jesus, and those laws, customs, devotional practices, and politics that had nothing to do with faith. He had come to believe that the whole structure of the Church could radically change without even touching the true basis of the Church itself. You could dispose of all its colleges, universities, hospitals, orphanages, institutions, agencies, and even its code of law, and you would not have even touched the Church, because those things are not the Church. They are merely the ways the Church has chosen to express its mission in the world. The essence of the Church lies far beneath the façade that is apparent to the world, David knew. Like the kingdom of God, it lives in the minds and hearts of its people whose faith can express itself in a thousand

different forms. And knowing this, David was determined to be an effective leader and go where he felt God
was leading him and his people.

The archbishop was concerned about David's intention to restructure his diocese in such a radical way and
hoped he could get him to be more sensible.

The two bishops met for dinner at L'Ecole. The
archbishop was a tall man, stately, and almost regal in
bearing, with a full head of white, wavy hair. Even
sitting at the table he was impressive. During the dinner, the two men sounded most civil in their conversation, and people in the restaurant would not have had
the slightest hint they were indulging in anything but
light talk over a very pleasant dinner. This polite recep-
tion was indicative of David's personality. He proved to
be a consummate diplomat, not giving in an inch on any
of his plans, but convincing the archbishop that he
would think over seriously his misgivings about his proposed changes.

The two men left on friendly terms. All David really
accomplished was to buy himself a little time. He knew
that as soon as he began to execute his ideas, there
would be another confrontation. His chancellor would
see to that.

During the course of the next few weeks, Father Ed
Marcel's dispensation arrived from the Vatican. That in
itself was momentous, as usually these things took
months and sometimes years to come through. David
glanced quickly over the stilted Latin text to see if the
Holy Father had kept his word. He had. The ordinary
demands required for the dispensation were noticeably
missing. David was gratified immensely. As simple as it

was the change was historic. The first step of David's plan had worked and the stage was now set for the next phase.

David sighed a silent prayer of thanks and immediately called Dick Franey to tell him the news and invite him to dinner for a strategy session before breaking the news to Ed Marcel. The night they met, David called the Holy Father to tell him of the dispensation's arrival and to thank him for facilitating the processing of the document. He also wanted to clear the next step with him. The Pope himself was eager for this experiment to work and receive a positive reaction from the people. David shared his strategy with the Holy Father and after some minor adjustments he approved, with the stipulation the affair be kept as low-key as possible.

A few days later David told Ed the news and invited him over to discuss the dispensation and what it meant in practical terms. He also wanted to share some thoughts about how they should next proceed.

"Ed, I can't tell you how happy I am that the dispensation came through," David told the priest by way of introduction, "and without all the ordinary demands. Do you still feel the same about going ahead with this, or are you having second thoughts?"

"Of course I feel the same, David," Ed responded. "I had thought this over thoroughly, and I am sure Maureen will be thrilled at the news."

"Ed," David said, getting down to business, "the next step may not be as simple. This is the first time in centuries we have had a chance like this, and I don't want to flub it. I fully realize some of our own will be horrified. They'll feel threatened and put all the pressure they can on their friends in high places to obstruct our plans, so it is essential we act prudently."

"David, I appreciate that," Ed remarked, "but it is my life and I don't want our new life together to be dictated by those . . . well, I won't say what I would like to say."

"I fully realize that, and I feel the same way," David countered, "but you also have to realize that what we are doing affects not just ourselves, but if we can pull it off, many others in the future. We will all have to be well disciplined. Otherwise, the whole thing can blow up in our faces and we will have lost the chance of the century. I don't intend to do that, Ed, and I don't intend to let you do it either. This is much more important than just you and Maureen. I have put myself way out on a limb for this, farther than you know, and I'm not going to let it fail. So, Ed, resign yourself to some restrictions."

"What do you propose, David?" Ed said in a more conciliatory tone.

"First of all, I have been thinking of late of restructuring the diocese, away from the rigid concept of parishes run by priests. I am considering letting the people control their own communities and freeing the priests to evangelize. It doesn't make sense to have our priests tied down to resaving the same souls week after week when there are millions of people desperately trying to find a meaning to life.

"I intend to set up a training program to teach our priests to bring the message of Jesus to a much wider audience. Once that is done, I'll have public relations people set up talks and programs at key centers around the diocese and invite the general public. There are so many people who have left the faith and many more who are unchurched. They should be our top priority. As shepherds we have to reach out to those people and offer them the healing message of Jesus. I know some of our priests are not suited for that kind of work, but you should be a natural, with your outgoing personality and your knowledge of Scripture, and your concern for people."

"You mean that's all I'm going to do?" Ed questioned, somewhat disappointed.

"What do you mean, 'all I'm going to do'? That's a big job, preaching the word of God. It was a full-time job for Jesus. You will have considerable free time between assignments, and you will be free to accept Mass assignments at various parishes as well. However, for the time being at least, I would like you to offer Mass only in outlying villages where there is a shortage of priests already. The people there will be glad to have Mass on Sunday, and you will be more than welcome by them."

"David, I don't think that's fair. It makes me into a second-class priest," Ed protested.

"Ed, you're being oversensitive. You can't have it all. We can't shove this down people's throats. Many are not ready for it, and if you go into big-city parishes, all you need is just one radical reactionary group, and they'll make life miserable for everyone. You'd end up regretting your rashness. I'm going to insist on this, Ed; there is no other way."

"Well, I don't like it, David, but I know you're on the spot as well as I am, and I do appreciate you sticking your neck out for me. I'll go along with it."

"One more thing, Ed," David said. "I think the fewer who know of this the better off we'll be."

"I understand," Ed agreed.

Then, handing Ed the dispensation, David told him, "Take it home, read it carefully, discuss it with Maureen to make sure you can live with it, and if you like you can call Dick Franey. He'll be glad to discuss the implications with you. Then, when you finish, you can sign it and give it back to me. I'll make sure it is routed to the proper office in the Vatican. That's important."

"What's the next step, David?" Ed asked.

"Stay put until you return the document. By then we will know just what to do. And pray." David shook Ed's hand and walked him to the door.

Later that same day Bill O'Donnell called with a progress report on the proposed clinic for his area. The whole neighborhood was ecstatic with the thought that they were going to get a clinic in the locality. The few Jewish people in the town were the first to respond and offer help. The various Protestant clergy and laypeople were also supportive, and the community at large, while having some questions as to the practicality of maintaining such an operation, generally thought it would be a boon to the area. A committee had already been formed to go ahead with the feasibility study, which they hoped to have completed by the end of the summer, with a full report on their findings.

David had been spending much of his time casually visiting the parishes all across the diocese, showing the same concern and interest in each as he did in Bill O'Donnell's. Some of the pastors and priests were on vacation, and it seemed they were always on vacation no matter when David called to arrange a visit, so he never saw them. But of those he saw, most were impressed with the openness of their new bishop.

The response of the people was always positive. In fact they were thrilled that the bishop was offering his help so they could do things in their community. What impressed them most was that David was not just interested in Catholics but was genuinely concerned with the whole community and all its people—and not for proselytizing reasons. He cared for people, and he wanted to be of service to everyone. Joshua had told him that Jesus saw the whole world as one family. If David was to imitate the Good Shepherd his concern should be all-inclusive, not just narrowly limited to his immediate flock. As a result David always insisted in his meetings with the pastors that they include people from the community when planning ventures for their neighborhood. One thing he felt strongly about was that each region have apartment complexes for the elderly, with nursing facilities attached, so the old folks would not have to go miles away from home when they needed a more protective environment. To send these people far from home and from all their friends was cruel.

Some parishes had high concentrations of children. It was important that centers be available for children to gather and play and do creative things. Another interest was mini-schools where kids having problems in their own schools could be tutored. David also believed there should be some hostels where children could go when they were facing desperate situations at home which they could no longer endure. Homes for other troubled people who find their circumstances unbearable was another priority. The diocesan director of social services could play a big part in coordinating all these services and programs, so they could be properly planned and placed where they would do the most good.

By the middle of the summer, the whole diocese was alive with activity. People's interest—and their faith— in their Church was renewed. More importantly, their faith in God was rekindled. Though it was not David's intention, contributions to the parishes and to the diocese skyrocketed, because people saw the money being used for their own communities. Young people showed a renewed interest in their Church because they could see their Church truly interested in them and not just because it could teach them religion.

Joshua was playing an ever-increasing role in helping David plan strategy. His ideas were practical and always showed deep concern for people. "God is concerned about His children, not about structures, which exist only to aid God's children," was a favorite expression of Joshua's, which he repeated endlessly. "Teaching God's children to love one another and helping them to work together to build caring communities is the great work of the Church," was another, and what he meant by "God's children" was everyone who was searching for God.

David did only what he felt he should do as a caring shepherd, and the community was responding. He began to receive invitations to speak at various Protestant churches, which he did with enthusiasm, and felt honored to do so. He also let it be known throughout the diocese that if ministers needed someone to cover for them when they went on vacation, the priests were to make themselves available if at all possible, not necessarily for the Eucharist, though even this should not be ruled out under certain rare circumstances. It was Joshua who talked him into that one; it was also something which he also talked to the Pope about. "Rare circumstances" was the Pope's contribution to the decision.

David's Sunday Mass at the cathedral was becoming a major event in the community. Almost every Sunday there was standing room only, but people did not seem to mind. Occasionally, Joshua would come and sit in the back quietly, absorbed in prayer, smiling approvingly at things David would say in his sermon. He never stayed, but David spotted him on one or two occasions walking down the steps afterward as he was leaving.

On one particular Sunday David gave an unusually touching sermon. It was toward the end of the summer, after he had already been to a number of Protestant churches for their services. "All my life I had looked upon the Catholic Church as the only legitimate vehicle for God's work on earth. I couldn't imagine God working through any other religious group. The Church was, after all, the one Jesus had founded, and He had to respect the mission He had given it. But working with Protestant people over the last few months, and to a lesser degree, over the years, I have witnessed a powerful presence of God in the lives of these people, a sensitivity to God's spirit. There is a humility on the part of Protestant clergy that, I must admit, I have not seen as much among our own. I have seen a deep and simple faith among so many Protestant people that it has been an inspiration to me. I have also been touched by the spiritual healings I have seen, and the genuine conversions to a holy life by people I have known to be not very religious. I witnessed the faith of a Protestant mother whose son was severely injured in an accident. The doctors had given up on the boy and told his mother there was nothing more they could do for him. The mother refused to give up and prayed constantly. I myself have seen that boy completely healed and back to work with no trace of the injury. I have seen a genuine willingness among Protestant ministers to draw closer to our Church in a humble attempt to respond to Jesus' prayer for unity, only to be held at a distance, and sometimes rebuffed by our priests, which hurt me deeply. I apologize for that.

"Participating in Protestant religious services, I was touched by their unrushed and deeply reverent liturgies that evidenced profoundly prayerful devotion. Yes, I have to say God is very much alive in the hearts of our Protestant people, and we can learn much from them and their beautiful Christlike spirit. In our striving for unity we will all benefit from the varied gifts God has given to each."

David's Mass at the cathedral each week was itself a graphic example of ecumenism. There were worshipers from every church in the diocese, Episcopalians, Presbyterians, Methodists, Quakers, Dutch Reformed, Pentecostals, Baptists, Assembly of God, and always a sprinkling of Jewish people who were comforted by David's deeply spiritual sermons. There was clearly one flock, a flock united in love and growing faith. David was well pleased. It was a true vindication of his belief that unity is a process that can begin only when it is allowed to start. If we wait until everyone is ready, it will never happen. Obstacles will always surface.

It was difficult to believe that David had been bishop for only a few months. The changes taking place were so widespread and so deep that one would think they could occur only after years of nurturing. It seemed to point so clearly to the fact that the world is ripe for people to follow the call of the Good Shepherd. All that remains is for the shepherds to heed the call.

CHAPTER 10

WHO can understand the awesome ways of God? Most of David's life as a priest had been ordinary, uneventful. He had fulfilled his responsibilities faithfully and conscientiously, but nothing dramatic ever happened. It was in many ways boring, until that fateful night after his ordination as bishop when the whole character of his life changed. Telephone calls, chance meetings, fortuitous events took place, seemingly unrelated, but which as time passed all came together like threads in a beautifully designed tapestry. David's insisting, for example, that pastors include community people in projects being planned had side effects hardly intended. People of various churches began working together; in time, they began worshiping together in each other's churches. Christians were even visiting friends' synagogues and vice versa. Protestant ministers invited David to their homes for lunch and dinner. When he spoke in their churches the places were packed. When their bishops or district superintendents first heard of these things they were suspicious, some even resentful, but as they came to know David personally their misgivings gave way to admiration. They saw him as a self-effacing and truly Christlike man of

105

God who genuinely cared for people and felt it was his duty as a bishop to draw all people together in Christ. That trait in David began to shine even more brightly as time went on.

In the course of the summer, David developed a close friendship with the Lutheran bishop, Donald Marxhausen. How this came about, however, was anything but pleasant.

Bishop Marxhausen was a huge man. He was as powerful emotionally and mentally as he was physically. As tall as David was, he was dwarfed by the presence of this man, whose nicknames were alternately "Big Bear" or "The German Shepherd." He was a friendly enough chap, and when he laughed the sounds rolled forth from deep within his huge frame.

One day Bishop Marxhausen, visibly upset, came to the chancery demanding to see David. It was a busy day and David was tempted to have his secretary arrange for an appointment until he realized who it was. He then went out to welcome him warmly and brought him into his private room rather than his office.

"This is purely business," Marxhausen blurted out. "I'm really upset." Then, as he made himself comfortable in the soft chair David motioned for him to sit in, he continued, "What in hell are you up to visiting my churches and playing up to my people?"

David fell back into his chair in shock, not a little embarrassed as half the chancery could hear every word from the bishop's booming voice.

"Bishop Marxhausen—" David started, before he was quickly interrupted.

"My name is Don," Marxhausen said, "you can call me that."

"Thank you," David answered. "Don, you have caught me off guard. I'm at a loss for words. I really don't know what I've done that's so horrible."

"Bishops don't make it a practice of cuddling up to parishes of other denominations," Don replied bluntly. "It's not cricket, and you've done it on more than one occasion. It's darn suspicious. I also don't like the idea of your priests asking our people to be on committees for your pet projects."

"Don," David tried to respond, "I can see what you mean, but, believe me, what I've done, I've done innocently. I had no ulterior motives or designs on your people. My mother was a Protestant, Lutheran to boot, and all my life I have been ashamed at the way so-called religious people treat one another. Until the day my mother died she was not allowed to receive Communion in the Catholic Church, even though her love for the Eucharist was deeper than that of many a Catholic I know. She was a much better Christian than my father, who had no trouble receiving Communion. That she should be denied was a sin, and it made me sad. I tried to justify it to her when I became a priest, but it broke my heart not to be allowed publicly to give my own mother Communion. Can you imagine anything so senseless? Europeans who live in all-Catholic countries can't understand that, nor the damage their narrow rules do to charity. Paradoxically, she was the one who taught me to respect the Pope, drumming it into my skull that he was still Peter and we should respect him.

"Ever since I was ordained, I made it a point of treating everyone as equal and making no distinctions among people in God's family. As bishop I instructed all the priests in the diocese to treat your people as our own. I felt in my heart that that was what Jesus did in His own day, and that was what He expects of us especially as His shepherds. I had no ulterior motives and no hidden agenda. I believe a bishop should be like Christ, and I believe that that's what He would do. Is there any other way? I could almost look upon you as a member of Christ's family," David said, taking his life into his hands, hoping Marxhausen had a sense of humor.

Don was caught off guard and grinned sheepishly while lowering his eyes, momentarily unable to look David in the eye.

"David, I'm embarrassed and ashamed. How could I have been so rash and so cruel in my judgment of you? You're not evil, you're just simple," he said half in jest and half in truth.

The two men laughed and hugged each other.

"I didn't know you're half Protestant," Don said while embracing David. "That explains a lot. I'm also sorry about your mother. That's what she gets for hanging around Catholics. And you're right, there is no other way for a bishop to treat people. I'm ashamed. It never occurred to me you could have the decency you've shown without having a motive behind it."

"No offense taken," David said good-naturedly. "My own people have a hard time understanding me. How could I expect an 'enemy general' to sit back while I raid his camp?"

Don gave out a deep belly laugh and said with good

humor, "Touché! I deserved that one. You're all right, David. I think I'm going to like you."

"That I should deserve such a cross," David said, smiling widely. "I think I could even like you, because I think my mother would be proud to meet a Lutheran bishop who's got what you have."

"What's that?" Don asked, curious.

"I don't dare put it in words. It might come out obscene," David said with a grin.

"I think I know what you were going to say," Don replied, with a knowing grin to match David's. "I agree. It's better if you don't say it. They said the same thing about Luther."

"Yes, you do have a lot in common," David said.

The crisis dissipated in the laughter of the two bishops' joking.

"Don, it's almost lunchtime," David said. "How about having lunch with us, myself and the staff?"

"That would be fun," Don replied.

Ever since that day the two bishops became best friends, inviting each other to their respective churches for services and programs. David invited Don to speak on numerous occasions at the cathedral. Don encouraged his own pastors to invite David to speak in their churches, which they did and which made David more popular than ever among Lutherans. Don even quipped about it while speaking in David's cathedral, remarking on how David was more popular with his people than he was.

Don's talks were always solid, his doctrine more substantial than that of many a Catholic priest. David encouraged his people to listen to what the Lutheran bishop said, saying that the Church, to remain faithful to Jesus, had to be in a constant process of reform. He also pointed out to his people that Lutherans themselves could learn a lot from Catholics and, indeed, were already putting things back into practice that they rejected in the past. The place of Peter in the Church was again very much in vogue in Lutheran discussions, so dialogue and worshiping together was good for everyone.

David's relationship with Don was the topic of conversation with the Pope on more than one occasion. David told him that their friendship had great potential. He also informed the Holy Father that they had shared services together frequently, with the cathedral packed on each occasion. Though it wasn't encouraged, many of Don's people come to Communion.

The Pope was annoyed at first—more annoyed that David told him than that he was doing it. He knew he was doing it anyway, but would have just as soon not have been told. David, however, wanted him to know. He intended to make an issue of these things to force discussion and bring about change.

"We have to be more flexible on the matter of intercommunion," he told the Pope respectfully. "In a society where there are so many baptized Christians practicing their faith sincerely, it seems hypocritical to think that only Catholics are worthy to receive Christ in the Eucharist. To officially and publicly exclude Christians of goodwill does more damage than whatever dubious good it accomplishes."

When the Pope objected, saying the Eucharist was a symbol of unity and that it should be allowed only when there was true unity, not merely an apparent unity,

David replied with all due respect that unity was a process. He believed the Eucharist could foster that process and accelerate it more than any other practice. There was no purity of belief among people of any of our denominations.

"Holy Father—I mean John," David said, "there was a priest in our diocese who helped organize a pilgrimage to Medjagorje with two Southern Baptist ministers not too long ago. You can imagine what a transformation that took for those two Baptist ministers to bring their people to a shrine of Mary. Well, when they arrived, the priest said Mass, and when the two ministers came up to receive Communion, the priest would not let them receive Christ. I was horrified when I heard of it. That shows a pettiness that strikes me as being most un-Christlike."

"David," the Pope said wearily, "I realize that, but I am so tired of all the arguing here over this issue that it is hard to know what to do without causing scandal of some kind. David, all I can say to you is be prudent. That's all I'm going to say. The Church will change in time on a lot of issues, but we all have to be patient, even myself, as the Church always moves slowly. When I came here I thought I was going to change the Church and steer a different course. When I realized how complicated it was, I had to discipline myself to be patient, hoping that in time I could make some little changes here and there and lay the foundation for those who would follow me. The Church is too big and vast and embraces too many cultures to make radical changes without causing revolutions."

David had won on another front, although the Pope

was clearly becoming concerned. Still, he knew David was right and, although he could not see making the changes on a worldwide scale, he could see a benefit in allowing a model to develop in a particular corner of the Church if it could be accomplished discreetly.

In the middle of all these Church matters, little everyday happenings wove themselves surreptitiously into David's life. Like the old hitchhiker David had invited to stay at his house. The man finally showed up one day. He was sitting on the front porch when David came home from the chancery.

"Bill, I thought you would never show up. I had expected you a long time ago. You are still welcome. Can you stay?"

"I never realized you were a bishop," the old man said. "I'm embarrassed to have inconvenienced you that day. The truck driver told me all about you. I stopped by today to return the money you loaned me."

David smiled. "That wasn't a loan; it was a gift. I want you to keep it. I really don't need it."

"I am grateful to you for helping me. I wasn't feeling very well, and I had fears that I might not make it to Pennsylvania. I bought some medicine with the money you gave me. It was a big help."

"Where are you staying tonight? Can you stay with me? You are still welcome," David repeated to the old man with a genuine warmth in his voice.

The man was ashamed, but he didn't turn down the offer. He knew he couldn't live in the streets. Perhaps if he had done it all his life, it would not be so bad, but to start living this way in his old age was too much for his frail body to sustain.

"Yes, Bishop, I would be honored if I could stay with you. I can work. I would be more than happy to work for you. I could keep the grounds for you and do odd jobs around the place, so as not to be a burden," the old man said with a humility that brought tears to David's eyes.

"Christ's visiting me could never be a burden to me," David said, half to himself, so that the man didn't quite hear him. "No, you will be no burden at all. There is plenty of room. The place is too big for one man anyway. There is a nice apartment on the side of the house that is separated from the rest of the building, so you can come and go at your leisure."

As David went into the house, he helped the old man with what few possessions he had, an old, worn duffel bag and a suitcase.

"Are you hungry?" David asked.

"I can wait, but I would like a glass of water," the man answered.

David took a glass from the cabinet, filled it with water, and gave it to his guest.

He then showed him the apartment, which was connected to the house by an enclosed walkway. The apartment was fully furnished, with a little kitchen, a dining room, a bedroom, and a living room. The living room had a good-size picture window that looked out on the meadow toward a distant hill. It was David's favorite room.

The two men were to become good friends. The old man got up early each morning and, though he was a Lutheran, set up everything for David to offer Mass, and attended each day. They compromised on who would make breakfast because David liked making it, since he never knew until after he finished Mass what he felt like eating.

That same afternoon, after he had shown Bill to his apartment, David went to work in his garden. All the crops had been planted and were looking green and healthy due to all the spring rain. Each day he could pick vegetables of one sort or another for supper. There wasn't much to do in the garden except weed. Joshua hadn't been around for a while, but he showed up this day and helped David weed. As usual they talked about issues that concerned them both. He told Joshua about Ed's case, and Joshua was certain it would work out as planned, if he moved carefully. He warned David, however, that there were still many who loved customs more than people.

David had been struggling a lot of late over the shortage of priests and the controversy surrounding the ordaining of women. He decided to ask Joshua how he felt about women being priests and why Jesus didn't pick women as apostles.

"The customs in those days wouldn't allow it. Men were not even supposed to talk to women in public. Jesus wasn't out to change the customs of the times but to give the message of salvation and plant the seeds for the future. It is up to wise leaders to recognize the limitations within which Jesus had to labor and not mistake those limitations as immutable doctrines. As Paul said, 'There is no distinction between Hebrew or Greek, male or female, slave or freeman.' All are one to Jesus."

"Should I push for that, then, when I talk with the Holy Father next time?" David asked his friend.

"David, David, go slowly. You can't change the

world overnight. As I said, even Jesus had to work within the constraints of his society."

"But it's an injustice."

"When God gives the call, it will be so obvious that the bishops won't be able to resist. Don't go out looking for occasions. But if someone should come to you and you see she is strongly called by God and is clearly anointed by God, then do what you know you must. But, remember, the initiative must come from God and not from you. Don't create crises and expect God to bail you out. You will be able to tell a genuine call. It is inspired by a gentle spirit and a quiet love that is willing to serve, not driven by anger or by a quest for power. When a person like that approaches you, you will know she is from God. Then you must act, but not before."

"Joshua, you're a shrewd one. You really know people, don't you?" David responded, amazed by Joshua's insightful answer.

"I know what is in people," was all that Joshua said in reply.

"Joshua, can you stay for supper?" David asked his friend.

"No, I think not. I have things to do. Thank you anyway," Joshua said graciously.

"Can I drive you somewhere?" David asked, curious as to where Joshua went when he left his house.

"Yes, if you like."

David stopped in the house for a few minutes and came out with a bag full of food from the kitchen to give to Joshua, then went to the garage to get his car. The two men drove off. Almost four miles down the road, Joshua directed David to turn off on a side road, a lonely country lane. As they approached an old abandoned barn, Joshua told David to stop there.

When Joshua was getting out of the car, some shaggy-looking men and women emerged from the barn, curious to see who was approaching.

"Don't be afraid, David. These are my friends. I would like you to meet them. This is our home," Joshua said with almost a sense of pride. "It is not unlike Bethlehem."

"Oh, my God," David cried in disbelief. "This is where you go when you leave my house?"

"Yes. What is wrong with it? These friends are dear to my Father. They have always been special to me. Come in and meet them."

David followed Joshua toward the barn. Others emerged from the open doorway, men, women, and a few children, all poorly dressed. Joshua introduced them all by name, telling them David was the bishop and was God's shepherd.

It was suppertime for the little group, and they sat down on the grass to share what they had received from their begging earlier in the afternoon. Joshua was happy to tell them he also had something to share with them and opened up the bag David had given him. No one had very much, a sandwich, an apple, an orange, a loaf of bread, a bottle of root beer soda. Joshua had a few pieces of roasted chicken, a couple of tomatoes, and a few rolls. He said a little prayer as they all sat around in two small circles, then passed the bag to the woman on his right. She took a piece of chicken and a tomato and a roll, and passed the bag to a man sitting next to her. As the bag was passed from one to another, David watched, spellbound. The bag never emptied. At least forty pieces of chicken came out of that bag, and half as many tomatoes, and rolls. When they passed the bottle of soda around the same thing happened. No one made a fuss. It was accepted as if it were quite ordinary. David couldn't believe his eyes.

"Joshua, what's happening here? I can't believe what I'm seeing," David said to Joshua.

"David, why should you be surprised? You of all people. Accept what you see." By that time the bag was next to David. A little boy offered it to him. He took it and thanked him.

Joshua motioned for David to take some. "They will be embarrassed if you don't eat with them. They are your children, David, the little ones of your flock. If they pray for you you will be truly blessed, for my Father hears their prayers. Cherish them, David. When I leave, take care of them. No one else sees any value in them, so to people without faith they are a nuisance."

"Joshua, my God, I can't believe what I am witnessing," David repeated in genuine disbelief. "They can't be just left to live like this. Who owns this farm? It's obviously abandoned. I'll find out tomorrow and have the charities director buy the place for the diocese. We can fix up the farmhouse and expand it so they can live there rather than in this barn. Maybe they can raise their own chickens and have a little farm, so they can grow their own food."

"That's a good start, David," Joshua said. "Some of them are not well and need care. You will be richly rewarded for whatever you do for them."

As they ate, some in the group talked excitedly. Others sat in silence. When the meal ended, the children came up to Joshua and hugged him. One little girl named Nancy came over and looked up into his eyes. Joshua bent down and placed his hands on her shoulders, saying as he did so, "Yes, little one, what can I do for you this evening?"

"Joshua, my friend Katie is sick. She's been shivering and cold all day long. Can you touch her and heal her like you did to me yesterday?"

Katie was standing off to the side, a pathetic little thing, thin, emaciated, her hair disheveled. Joshua looked over at her and with his finger beckoned for her to come to him. She walked unsteadily, hesitating with each step. When she reached Joshua he put his arms around her and kissed her on the cheek. She looked at him sadly.

"You haven't been feeling well today, my little friend?" he asked.

"No, Joshua," she answered. "I've been so cold all day long. I can't get warm. Can you make me better?"

"Yes, little one," he said as he cradled her head in his hands. "Be healed, and feel the warmth and joy of God's love in your heart."

The girl looked into Joshua's eyes, and a change came over her immediately. She kissed him and thanked him. Nancy also gave Joshua a big kiss for making her friend better. The two girls ran off together.

David watched in silent amazement. His own life would never be the same after that. He took leave of Joshua and said good-bye to the others and drove off, promising to come back to visit them again.

All the way home his mind swirled in a whirlwind of

thoughts and ideas. He felt guilty coming back to his cozy, comfortable home, while Joshua and those home-less people lived in such squalor. The guilt, however, inspired him to do whatever he could to alleviate those frightful conditions. There must be other places around just like that. He would have his people check with the utility company and ask if their meter readers couldn't help identify them. They go all over and know where everyone lives. That would be the most efficient way of locating them with a minimum of delay.

By the time David arrived home, his houseguest had found the dishes, prepared supper from the food defrost-ing on the counter, and was ready to serve it. David was surprised. Bill apologized for barging into David's quar-ters, but hoped he had been helpful by preparing sup-per. He realized David had been delayed. But David did not mind at all. In fact he was grateful.

During supper, Bill told David more of his fasci-nating life story. It gave David an entirely different perspective on the homeless people who wandered the streets. He knew many of them were troubled souls, or alcoholics, but he now knew of a whole other type of street person with a sense of pride and self-worth, who in no way wanted to be in the streets, but was forced there by economic necessity and by a public pol-icy that had little concern for the plight of these for-gotten people.

After supper the old man excused himself and went to his apartment. He was used to retiring early and rising early. It was a habit he got himself into years ago while living at home on his family's little farm where he had to rise early to tend the animals.

David read for a while, then planned for the next day. It was difficult for David to plan his schedule, because his secretary and staff received all the phone calls and requests for interviews. To be a good shepherd and not just an administrator, he felt it was important for him to be accessible to his people, and particularly his priests, when they were hurting or needed him. David was good at that. Now he determined to take more personal control of his agenda.

The first thing he wanted the next day was for the social service director to check into the status of the abandoned farm and take steps to purchase it. Sure enough, he found that the farm was abandoned. The old people who had owned it died; they had no family. The property was available for taxes. David was fortunate. He made arrangements to have the taxes paid and the title conveyed to the diocese, with instructions to his staff to have the place cleaned up and the farmhouse renovated and readied for occupancy by Joshua's homeless family.

David found out in time that there were pockets of homeless in other places around the diocese. He contacted the relevant parishes to tell them of his concern for these people and asked if they would work with him in doing the same as he did with the abandoned farm. Some were reluctant but eventually all cooperated, especially when David offered funds to help offset the expense. Buses were obtained to transport the people from place to place; David felt it was important to treat them as humans with the same dignity as others who had more political clout. Unexpected support for the project came from David's newfound friend, Bishop

Marxhausen. When he heard what David was doing he called and asked why he didn't ask him to help. David told him he was impossible and never dreamed of asking him. "See, you'll ask my people, but you won't ask me. Aren't I human?" he asked in his customary grumpy fashion.

"I'd be delighted to have you help. Your money is as good as mine. Why don't you come down for lunch and we can plan our next move," David told him.

"Would you mind if I bring a friend? He's the Episcopal bishop," Don asked with a little hesitation in his voice.

"Not at all, as long as he's got some money he wants to spend."

"See you at noon," Don said, then hung up.

David had a considerable amount of unfinished business to take care of before noon, and worked double-time to finish it.

The first matter concerned a number of other reports about priests refusing to baptize babies because their parents were not frequent churchgoers. Even after his directive went out with detailed guidelines, these priests still remained inflexible. Some of them were even encouraged by certain chancery officials to adopt this hard line. David was furious. To him this was not only un-Christlike, it could not be tolerated. There were other, more gentle ways to handle these situations.

David called a meeting of the officials he knew were involved and minced no words in insisting they either follow his directives or take another job. "I can tolerate individuals here being treacherous toward myself, but I will not tolerate my staff being cruel and un-Christlike with the people. That is unforgivable," David said, looking straight at Charles as he said it. Charles turned purple.

This was one of the few times David had shown his anger. It was not a nice thing to see, because David had a frightful temper. Thankfully, however, it never stayed with him very long. He didn't stew over things. He acted immediately, addressed the cause of the anger, then became his normal relaxed self again.

Before the meeting ended, he directed the officials to call back the priests involved and instruct them to make peace with the families concerned and to follow the guidelines issued a few months earlier.

David was also getting reports of religious education directors using the same bullying tactics with children and their families. "What is it," David thought, "that makes religious people so damnably nasty in the way they feel they have to treat people? Some can be so nice and others have to be so dictatorial and self-righteous toward others."

One religious education coordinator, a sister who had always managed to wheedle her way into administrative positions, was downright unpleasant in the way she treated people. When Jesus told the apostles not to be like the important people of this world who love to lord it over their subjects and make their importance felt, it almost seemed that Jesus had this particular woman in mind.

She was determined everyone was going to do things her way, and she could be vicious and cruel when anyone dared oppose her, but in such a devious way that only those who knew her well could see her vicious strategy. She could quote Scripture like a master, always with a self-promoting agenda, of course. She would undermine even priests who dared to oppose her. David had had experiences with her in the past, and she had done things behind his back that caused him untold grief. He had tried to talk to her about it, but she was all oil and balm in convincing him he had made a big mistake in thinking she could ever do such a thing. She never dreamed he would ever become bishop.

Now she was up to her old tricks again. She had been running her religion program for the public school students as if it were a scholarship school, with textbooks, homework assignments, penalties for missing classes, and rigid, authoritarian regulations even for the parents. A few absences and the child was expelled from the program, in spite of the greater damage such cruel treatment could have. Even the volunteer teachers lived in fear of her wrath. Many people were literally driven from the parish by the unkindness of this one woman, with her stranglehold on the parish and the parish council. With all the money given in the Sunday collection, she still charged arbitrary fees. She controlled everything and everyone, and no one would dare question her authority. And all this in the name of the gentle Christ, the Good Shepherd, who was so solicitous of the bruised and hurting sheep.

David was determined to rid the diocese of this kind of hurtful practice which, though not common, was not rare either.

"Joan," he said to one of his secretaries, "would you please call Sister Ellen Farraghan and tell her I would like to see her here at the chancery tomorrow morning at nine o'clock? She'll probably give you a thousand reasons why she can't come, but tell her I insist."

While he was talking on the phone, the two bishops arrived at the chancery. They were right on time. David walked out to greet them rather than have them wait to be announced.

"David," Don Marxhausen said in introducing his companion, "this is Allan Rainville. I'm sure you know he's the Episcopal bishop of the area."

"David Campbell," David said by way of introduction. "I'm delighted to welcome you here. I've heard many good things about you from our late bishop. He thought very highly of you, and I'm honored that you grace us with your visit, though I can't help but suspect your judgment by the company you keep," David ended in jest.

Don laughed. "He's started already," Don interjected. "He didn't give me a welcome like that." Then, turning to David, he said, "Don't worry, David, I already told him about our first encounter, and was properly chastised for my big mouth."

Allan Rainville was a handsome man, sturdier built than David and more athletic in appearance, though not quite as tall as David. He was, of course, small by comparison to Don Marxhausen. The men were clearly compatible, a rare combination for three bishops who happened to be located in the same area.

"David, you're as gracious as all my people say you are," Allan said. "I've heard nothing but superlatives about the sermons you've been giving in our churches. My people love you."

David brought his guests into the dining room where the staff was already gathering and introduced everyone. They all sat down, David directing Don, since he was the biggest, to sit in his place at the head of the table—that chair was the sturdiest. After David offered grace, the cook brought out a large tureen filled with steaming homemade chicken soup.

This was the first of many meals the three bishops were to have together. In time they were to confer with each other on practically every issue that emerged as a topic of the day. On most things they agreed. On some things they had strong differences but knew when to back off and settle on points about which they could agree. They were all strong men with equally strong opinions, and though their views could be widely divergent they could still be best of friends. That is what made their relationship so rare and so refreshing.

By the end of the meal, the Episcopal bishop had been drawn into helping with the team adopting the homeless. The three men went into David's private room to work out details of the plans to provide services for those unfortunates. David told the bishops about Joshua and asked if they would be interested in meeting him. They agreed and decided they would follow David out to the farm when they finished their discussion.

When they arrived at the abandoned farm, Joshua was sitting under a tree telling stories to the children. They were such pathetic sights but became so beautiful in the attachment they had to Joshua. They sat spellbound on the ground as he spoke to them.

As the three men approached, the children turned to see the strangers. Joshua stood up to greet them. David introduced everyone. Joshua was as gracious as ever. The children ran off as the men sat down on logs and talked.

Don kept watching Joshua, not knowing what to make of this apparently simple man. Allan was attracted by the sensitivity of his manners and his sharp awareness of all that was said. Nothing passed his attention.

Curious as to what would attract a man of Joshua's refinement to such people as the homeless, Don asked him outright what he saw in them.

"The same thing Jesus saw in the street people of His own day. They are hurting and there are few who care. It is not easy to go through life unloved and with the feeling you are not really wanted by society. These people touch the heart of God because they have no one to love them," Joshua said.

"Are they different than anyone else that God should care more for them?" Don continued, not because he didn't care, but because he was trying to find out what made Joshua tick.

"They are human," Joshua answered. "They are God's children, they sin, they love, they struggle, like everyone else, but they have been unjustly deprived of those things people need to survive. God intended that those He blessed care for those without; when they don't, God Himself reaches out to them."

At that point a little boy came running up to Joshua and cuddled up to him, resting his head on his shoulder. Joshua put his arm around him as he continued talking to his visitors. The boy was happy just to feel the comfort of his presence, not needing to say anything.

"Take this little boy, for example," Joshua continued. "He's a bright boy. He has nothing. Whose fault is it that he is deprived of an education? Is it his? Is it his parents', who do not have the money to buy clothes and shoes or books and pencils to equip him for school, or a home to provide for him a place to study? It is not the fault of God, who lavishes His riches on others so they can pass His blessings to people like this. When they greedily keep for themselves what God has blessed them with to help others, then you have the homeless and the starving. God has given them more than enough food to feed the world. If people starve, it is because others don't care. Do you think it will go well on Judgment Day with those who have built their casinos and their castles and amassed their riches by shutting their hearts against the hurting masses of humanity?"

"I guess you are real, Joshua," Don said, impressed with Joshua's sensitivity. "You're echoing what Jesus already said. It will annoy people today just as it did when He said it way back then."

David just watched and listened. Allan said little, but he was obviously intrigued. He could see beneath the surface of this apparently simple man and sensed there was much more to him than he was willing to reveal.

Changing the subject, Joshua shifted the conversation back to the three men. "I am glad you three found each other and have become friends. There was nothing that troubled Jesus more as He was departing than that His followers would tear apart God's family. Realizing this, His last prayer with the apostles was that they would all be one. You can help to bring that about if you keep your hearts focused on what is important to God."

The three were all caught off guard. You don't expect to hear a layman talking about what is important to God. You don't even hear clergy showing much concern for what God really wants. They are concerned about what is expedient for the logical, political working of the kingdom on earth.

"How do you mean that, Joshua?" David asked in an attempt to break the uneasy silence that followed Joshua's remark.

"Very simply," he replied. "You are all shepherds, and good shepherds. There are many ways you can work together. As time goes on, if you are open to God's spirit, He will guide you along paths you never dreamed possible."

Joshua was in territory where not even clerics felt comfortable, so the subject quickly changed.

"How many people are living here?" Don asked, directing the question to no one in particular.

Joshua answered. "The number varies from between twenty-five to thirty-five. Sometimes people come and just stay overnight then move on. This group has a good reputation, so strangers feel safe when they stay with us." Joshua was a relative newcomer and not a permanent part of the group.

Their curiosity satisfied, and since it was already late in the afternoon, David's friends signaled their need to leave. David thanked Joshua for his time and courtesy. After exchanging pleasantries, the three bishops left, Don and Allan heading back to the city and David going home, since it was already late in the afternoon.

11

DAVID arrived at the chancery early the next morning to finish writing memos for the staff before they came to work. At nine o'clock sharp, Sister Ellen arrived for her appointment. David ushered her cordially into his office and couldn't have been more gracious in the way he handled a very delicate situation. Unable to be cruel to anyone, David told her her contract as director would not be renewed, but since she had such great ability in a number of areas, he would like for her to choose one of a list of four possible assignments, none of which involved her being in charge of people. The woman left David's office fully aware of David's reasons, though not a word of the precise nature of those reasons was discussed. She was not happy with being fired, which she knew was what David really did, though with such finesse that she left his office with pride intact, which she rarely had the decency to do to others with whom she had dealings.

After Sister Ellen left, David had an appointment with Ed Marcel. During the interval since their last meeting David had arranged for Ed to enter a workshop on evangelism. It was not a very involved course, but something new for a Catholic priest who had been

trained in scholastic philosophy and theology. Ed, however, turned out to be a natural as an evangelist. He not
only enjoyed the workshop but hadn't been able to wait
to get started on his new assignment.

David himself was impressed with what he had seen
in Ed since his return from the workshop and began to
realize that this new venture could have dramatic potential in the Church's effort to bring Jesus to people,
not just the unchurched but those faithful ones who
were so in love with the Church that they never got to
know Jesus.

Convinced that Ed was ready for his new work as an
evangelist, David had alerted the public relations people
to begin the promotion work to insure a respectable attendance. The first few had been only moderately attended, but as Ed's reputation spread, so had the size of
his audiences, which previously numbered in the hundreds, but now were counted in the thousands.

Ed arrived late and was all apologies. "David, I am so
sorry for being late. I really have no excuse."

"That's understandable, Ed," David said. "We are
all late sometimes. Have a seat," he said, nodding toward one of the soft armchairs reserved for guests.

"Well, tell me all about your new work. Do you like
it?" David said.

"Like it? David, I love it. You can't imagine what's
been happening. I feel that this is the first time in my
whole priestly life that I have really done a priest's work.
You're a genius. I brought Maureen with me the last
few times and she is totally involved with the work.
There are others who come with her so she doesn't have
too high a profile, but she is really a big help, as well as

a tremendous moral support to me. David, I can't thank you enough."

"Ed, what about Mass?" David asked. "How have you solved that problem since I relieved you of your work in the parish?"

"So far I have had no problems," Ed responded enthusiastically. "I have been helping out in two mountain villages on weekends. Maureen comes with me. Nobody asks any questions. Some of the people know me. A few are aware of the situation and understand. They are grateful I come. They haven't seen a priest in months, so they are delighted when I show up because they really miss confession and the Eucharist."

"I am happy with what I've heard so far about your talks," David told Ed. "The people love them. Even the public relations people are impressed and suggest I free more priests to do that kind of work. Do you have any suggestions as to what we can do to help?"

"Yes," Ed replied. "You might want to set up workshops to prepare the local parishes for their follow-up work. The most I can do in my talks is get people to commit themselves to the Lord. Once they do that they have to have a support community to plug into. If the parishes are not ready to accept them, we will really have a problem."

"Good idea!" David said as he continued to jot some notes.

David was happy with the way his plans for Ed were taking shape. He hoped and prayed that this experiment would work. If it did it would open the door for more of the same, especially if the evangelical work was successful in bringing a goodly number of people to Christ.

"Ed," David said in a thoughtful tone, "what would you think of my recalling some of the priests who have left and asking them if they would be interested in doing this kind of work?"

"If you got the right ones, I think it would be great," Ed responded. "I think you might want to start with just a few to see how it goes. There is one fellow I would really love to have working with me. He left a few years ago, but I've never met a priest like him. He's a natural. His name is Andre Constantin. He has four children, but people tell me he is still a priest right to his finger-tips. It's a sin they let that man go."

"Well, if you can track him down, I am willing to give him a try," David said. "If you think of any more let me know, and we will consider each one individually."

David couldn't wait to tell the Pope of the success of their scheme, knowing it would bring him the kind of assurance he was hoping for in allowing the experiment.

After the meeting with Ed, David was expecting Bill O'Donnell and some of his committee with a progress report.

The committee, which was half Protestant, was enthusiastic with the progress made so far. The architectural designs were finished, and the necessary approvals were granted by the various state and local government boards as well as the health department. The whole community was solidly behind the project, and everyone was awaiting David's approval for the ground breaking. David was delighted. Everything seemed to be going like clockwork.

Reports from some other projects David had encouraged around the diocese indicated they were also making good progress. David could not be happier.

His program to wed the schools with industry was not as simple, however. Later on the same day after his meeting with Bill O'Donnell, David met with Tom Langan. Tom was president of Aerobotics, a high-tech corporation that was a subsidiary of one of the biggest corporations in the country. Tom was sold on David's concept of industry sharing responsibility for education and had most of his own people enthusiastic about the idea. Still, they were having a difficult time interesting their board of directors in the project. The chairman of the parent company, however, had given the go-ahead to start the project, although he would not make a permanent commitment until they could evaluate its long-term benefits. The bottom line was that they would go ahead with the plan but could not guarantee not pulling out somewhere down the line if they felt it was not in the company's best interests.

David was convinced enough of the inherent value of the program that he was willing to accept a partial commitment, feeling that in the long run the company would see its value even from a selfish point of view.

Tom informed David they would be able to send teachers and administrators into the schools by late summer. Brochures would be available for parents and students in a few weeks so they could familiarize themselves with the wholly new approach to their education. The children should find it exciting because the company would be sending in sophisticated computers and robotics equipment that would be part of the courses. Those who would benefit most would be the students who would not be going to college and who had a talent for practical mechanical operations. They could be adequately trained in a couple of years and upon graduation could go directly to Aerobotics for immediate employment.

There was still much planning and coordinating with the existing faculties and administrations to assure a smooth transition. The company would be footing the bill for the programs and classes it would be providing as well as for the teachers and administrators of their division of the school. Eventually, if the plan worked out, the company would assume more financial responsibility for the operation of the school. It would be no longer a Catholic school, but an ecumenical school with the various denominations providing instructors to teach their children religion.

In other areas of the diocese schools were in various stages of development of the new program, but all seemed to be moving forward. It was not easy to get a new concept like this started, so in most of the places the plan would not be fully implemented for another year or so. David was particularly grateful to the people at Aerobotics because they would be providing a working model for others to observe and analyze. However, his superintendent of schools was the one man who deserved much of the credit for the success of the operation: he was responsible for all the tedious negotiations with the many companies involved. David fully appreciated his loyalty and total dedication to the project.

That afternoon David left early to spend time in his garden. The tomatoes were ripening. The corn was almost ready. Other vegetables he had been harvesting for the past three weeks. He was thrilled to be able to share his harvest with Joshua's homeless friends. They were beginning to look to him for support and, more frequently as the days went on, for medical care. All the papers had been processed for the purchase of the abandoned farm, and the contractors were busy with the renovations of the house and other buildings.

Joshua still made his appearances at David's, showing up whenever David especially needed him, discussing matters that sometimes were beyond David's comprehension. The human mind, no matter how sharp it may be, can cope with only so much before it shuts down and refuses to process any more material. That was happening to David. The radical changes that had been occurring were gigantic in scope and required so much attention that he was beginning to feel he just couldn't absorb anything else. Joshua's presence and understanding made it possible to further expand his view and renew his strength. Joshua seemed to move with such ease in areas that to him were ordinary, but to the limited human mind were nothing less than sublime.

David enjoyed his time alone in the garden. He was getting weary of all the complications of his new work as bishop. He needed this quiet time more than ever. His houseguest stayed by himself and never disturbed him. In fact David rarely even knew he was home. In the beginning Bill used to get up early and have breakfast with David, but it was becoming more difficult for him, especially if he didn't sleep well the night before. David would look in on him to make sure he was all right. Since David's schedule was so erratic, Bill never counted on him for dinner, so they ate separately most of the time, though sometimes they would eat together, particularly on feast days.

Joshua stopped over frequently while David was working in the garden. They worked together and talked, Joshua on one occasion sharing his vision of the Lord's kingdom as a garden that is forever being renewed. "If a farmer plants the same crops each year he wears out the soil," Joshua pointed out, "and it is good for nothing. A wise farmer will change the crops each year so the soil can replenish its strength. It is the same with the kingdom of God on earth. The people must be continually renewed."

On another occasion he compared the kingdom of God to a wise shepherd who understood his sheep. "As times change, people's experiences change, and it is difficult for them to accept outworn practices. A wise shepherd will realize that his people are hurting and from his resources will make adjustments. It is only a stupid shepherd who will keep applying the same formula no matter what the circumstances, saying, 'It was good for us when we were children, it is just as good now.' As people's experiences change, practical applications of Jesus' teachings must also change if they are to make sense."

"But Jesus' teachings are changeless," David objected.

"They are changeless in their principles, but not in their application," Joshua retorted. "Take, for example, Jesus' gift of forgiveness, which He shared with the apostles. That is unchanging. How it is administered can vary as people's needs change. When people stop

accepting forgiveness in traditional form, it expresses a
clear message: That form has lost its meaning for them.
The whole Christian world can't be wrong. Find another way. At that point the form must change. Not to
change shows an unhealthy love of ritual and contempt
for people's spiritual needs."

"Joshua, you are confusing me," David said in an
almost discouraged tone. "Don't you think I have done
enough already? How far do you expect me to go? I am
in trouble as it is."

Joshua laughed. "I am not referring to you, David.
You are listening to God, and, as you can see, it is
reaping its rewards. All the flocks are coming together.
I merely share with you my vision of what could be. In
time you will see your way. You are tired now because
you have done so much in so short a time. Do not be
discouraged."

"Joshua, come in and have supper with me," David
said with insistence in his voice. "At least a bite, then
I'll drive you down to your friends. I picked up some
things so they could have a cook-out."

"I guess I can't refuse when you put it that way,"
Joshua responded.

"I have a man living in the house with me," David
said. "I picked him up hitchhiking one day and invited
him to come stay with me. He's a nice old fellow. I'd like
you to meet him."

The old man was just coming back from the field
where he had been taking a walk. David could see he
had weeded the flower beds and under the shrubs around
the house. They were perfectly manicured.

The three met at the back door. "Nice job you did

with those flower beds, Bill," David said appreciatively. "I haven't bothered with them for a long time. My father used to love doing that, but I've let them go. Bill, this is Joshua, a friend of mine."

The two men greeted each other. Joshua looked into Bill's eyes and saw the long years of hurt and loneliness. Bill was touched by Joshua's look of compassion. He felt a sense of awe and peace just being in his presence. David led them into the house, and cooked supper.

The next day, David had another phone call from the archbishop. He called him back as soon as he went into his office.

"Hello, Bishop," David said in a friendly manner.

"Hello, David," the archbishop responded in a businesslike tone. "What is all this talk I'm hearing about you allowing a married priest to continue functioning as a priest? Is it true?"

"As a matter of fact, Bishop, it is," David answered.

"What in God's name are you trying to accomplish, David? Don't you realize that's going against all the rules? It's in direct violation of canon law."

"I'm very much aware of that, Bishop, but I am also aware, fully aware, that this man has a calling from God to the priesthood, and I intend to be obedient to God."

"David, you can't be obedient to God by violating canon law," the archbishop answered flatly.

"Canon law was drawn up by canon lawyers. They can make mistakes and be unresponsive to God just like anyone else. There are many things in canon law that are not exactly in the spirit of Christ. That's why they change it so often. Does that mean that I have to follow them when I recognize in a given situation that the law doesn't apply?"

"David, you can't take the law into your own hands."

"I am not. It was simply clear what I had to do, and I did it."

"Does that mean you have no intention of retracting what you have done?"

"Yes."

"Well, if that's the case, I will have no alternative but to report the matter to the pronuncio."

"You are one hell of a colleague, Bishop!" David exploded. "You know full well you have no obligation to do that unless you choose to. If it means that much to you politically to betray a fellow bishop, then you are not the man I thought you were. It is bad enough I have one Judas stalking me, without having a fellow bishop doing the same. Whatever you do, I will stand before God, alone if I have to, knowing that I protected a calling that He gave to one of my priests. God will judge in the end who was right. I can wait until then. It means more to me to do what is right before God than even being a bishop, if it comes to that. So do what you must. I couldn't care less."

The two men hung up in anger.

The rest of the morning was tense. David was never one to oppose authority. To find himself in this situation with the archbishop was, to say the least, distasteful. Moreover, his relationship with his chancellor was getting worse. On the surface, David was courteous to him, the way he felt Jesus was to Judas, but inside he found it much more difficult to be Christlike. He had bitter feelings for the man and felt ashamed and guilty for the feelings. What made it so difficult was the fact that the chancellor was David's right hand, and they had to work on all the important diocesan matters together. David struggled day and night to be kind and forgiving toward the spiteful man, but even with his best efforts he was only slightly successful. He felt no satisfaction in it, though what he had accomplished was heroic.

His secretary, Jim Mohr, found out one day what Charles was up to, and felt it his duty as David's confidential secretary to tell him. He was shocked that David knew and amazed that he could be so kind to him. Jim wasn't as disciplined as David. He couldn't turn the other cheek. He confronted Charles one day and blasted him for being a Judas, telling him without mincing words that he had nothing but contempt for him.

Charles's defense was that he was protecting the Church and being loyal to Christ. "The Church is sacred," he said, "and this man is destroying it and everything in it that's sacred. I can't in conscience stand idly by and not do something about it."

"I suppose that's what Judas felt about Jesus, too, that he was destroying all that was sacred," Jim replied caustically. "And others in Jesus' day felt the same way about Jesus, and that they were doing God a favor by killing him. I suppose your kind will always exist. Doesn't it ever occur to you that the bishop might be a saint, and that you could possibly be doing a horrible injustice?"

"No," Charles shot back, "it is too absurd to even consider. What he is doing to the Church is evil. No saint would do such a thing."

Since that exchange Jim couldn't stand the sight of the chancellor and absented himself from meetings they were both supposed to attend. David tried to encourage him to be more understanding, but Jim couldn't.

That night David called the Vatican. The Pope had already heard the rumors about David and told him.

"I don't know where they came from, David, but they have already alerted important people here," the Holy Father told him with deep concern.

"Holy Father—I mean, John. You know, I'm never going to get used to calling you by name. I don't intend to let what they say or do bother me. I do care what you think because I respect you, but I feel I have to follow what I know in my heart God wants me to do. What happens to me is irrelevant."

"I admire you, David. I wish I could have been like you all my life, but I probably wouldn't be here now if I was. I agree with you in my heart, David, but I am also concerned for you. I am willing to go along with what you are doing, because I know someday those things will have to be done, but I also know myself, David. I am not a strong man. I have been trained as a diplomat all my life, and diplomats know only how to compromise. I fear, David, that one day you are going to be the victim of a compromise. I won't be able to hold out against these people if they all agree that you are creating a serious disturbance in the Church. I hope you realize that. As much as I love you, I am not going to be able to stand up against them."

"I realize that, John," David said respectfully. "I realized that all along. It doesn't bother me as long as I can follow my conscience. I appreciate the confidence you have placed in me in allowing me to take the steps I have. I also realize that what I am doing is putting you on the spot, which is not really fair, and that someday you are going to have to face the prefects of the congregations to answer for what I am doing, and that you will be forced to make a decision. I have already considered that, and when it happens I can accept it. I will still love you and respect you for allowing me to follow my conscience and set in motion that which cannot be reversed. I am trying to be prudent. Be patient with me, because there are some things that are happening that I will share with you soon. I think we are on the verge of something wonderful. Please keep your mind open to whatever might transpire. I'll keep you informed."

"David, you frighten me," the Pope responded. "Don't you ever give up?"

"How can we when God is obviously working with us?" David answered.

The Pope gave David his blessing but again warned him to be careful, especially of people in his own house. David thanked him and promised to be prudent.

12

TOWARD the end of the summer David took a few days off with old classmates from seminary days. They had kept contact through the years, though most of them were from other dioceses. A hardy, good-natured crew, they liked the rugged coast of Maine, and spent whatever free time they could scrape together gathering at a house they had bought on the rocky coast above Boothbay Harbor. Far away from people and commitments and telephones, they were able to completely relax and forget the worries and responsibilities of their jobs. David always returned totally rejuvenated after his days at the coast. Being bishop, however, David had to keep in frequent contact with the chancery, which meant his corresponding secretary and Charles. Charles was in his glory when David went away because everyone had to come to him for day-to-day decisions.

While on vacation David and the others just loafed. They took turns making breakfast in the morning, then would pray their office together, the Psalms and readings from Scripture and the early Fathers. The rest of the day they whiled away by taking walks along the coast, or playing cards or volleyball, or just sitting around reminiscing about old times. At night they would either go out to dinner or cook out on the rocks overlooking the ocean.

On his return to his diocese, David plunged back into his work. The staff had been accustomed to David's efficiency as a fellow worker before, but now there was an intensity and a hurry to everything David did. Everyone wondered what the rush was. It was almost as if David felt he did not have much time and had to accomplish everything by some fast-approaching deadline.

Ed Marcel's evangelizing work was encouraging in its results. David attended one of his talks to see firsthand why people were so captivated.

He had heard evangelists in the past and was never impressed. Ed's approach was different. He was able to communicate his personal sense of Christ to his audience. He was preaching not a Church or a religion or a scripture—he was preaching a living Christ. It left his audience mesmerized. This was what they had been looking for all their lives. They had known religion before. Even for those well versed and well practiced in it, there was still something essential missing. This was it, an intimacy with God. Ed's approach introduced them to a Jesus and a God who was real, who could understand the frailty of human beings because He made them that way and was not shocked at seeing His children acting human, even though the self-righteous would look down on them.

David was impressed. He decided then and there that this was the work he wanted his priests to do. Get them out of the parishes to bring Jesus to the people, a real, living Jesus.

The first team David handpicked. There were thirty of them, men and some women who had solid training in Scripture and spirituality and already a good sense of Jesus. He arranged for Ed to train the team and teach them his technique for inspiring people to a greater intimacy with Jesus and a deeper sense of God in their lives.

David had discussed the program with Don Marxhausen and Allan Rainville, and also with the Methodist bishop, Jim Dorsey, but they weren't ready for it yet. They were, however, open enough to the idea to offer their churches for the talks. That was a great help, because David did not want people to get the idea he was just trying to corral people into his church to push up the numbers. Furthermore, all these churches scattered throughout the diocese formed an accessible network for people to gather for the talks.

The project was heavily promoted in all the communities throughout the area, and everyone was invited. The launching date was September. The whole team started on the same day, sent to every nook and cranny of the territory. The response was overwhelming. Not even David could have imagined the turnout, including people who had never been inside a church before. Many came out of curiosity, but many because they were willing to give it one last chance, hoping that this just might be different from what they were used to. Even the curious were impressed.

Many people finally found what they were looking for, not a watered-down, superficial religion, as some would call it, but a God who made sense and a God who cared, a God who inspired them to a higher way of living, but who could be understanding when people fell along the way.

The speakers were invited to return practically every place they had appeared. David was encouraged. He expanded the teams. He also assigned the men to exchange pulpits with their fellow priests so the Catholic congregations could be reintroduced to Jesus. His Protestant bishop friends were impressed and asked if their people could be part of the team. David was delighted that this was becoming a cooperative effort. Individual pastors from other denominations timidly asked if they could join in either by providing host churches or as members of the preaching teams. The project exploded into an ecumenical bonanza.

One of the happy side effects of David's approach as shepherd was the response from fellow bishops at the Bishops' Conference, held a little over a month after the trip to Maine. Word had spread fast about all the changes David had initiated in his diocese. The bishops were curious and cornered him at the conference, plying him with every imaginable question: Was he getting flak from the Vatican over the married priest still working as a priest; wasn't he worried about diluting the theology of Christ by concentrating so much on the humanity of Jesus; wasn't he afraid that by having the priests evangelizing in this way, he was encouraging people to find spiritual comfort outside the Catholic Church and outside the sacraments? David allayed their fears, telling them that church attendance had doubled, and that the number of converts had demanded augmented teams of catechists to train the large numbers. And no, he had

had no trouble so far over his married priest still preaching the word of God.

Most of the bishops admired what David was doing. Some had been doing similar things in their own dioceses but quietly and as carefully as possible so as not to arouse reactionaries who were only too ready to turn in their bishops to the modern equivalent of the Inquisition. A handful of bishops asked David if he might be willing to send some of his men out to train priests and others in their dioceses. He was more than willing.

There were, however, some bishops who were close to Archbishop O'Connell who had heard all about David before they got to the conference. They ignored him and had nothing good to say about David to any who would listen to them. David felt their hostility. They made no effort to hide it. He rather predicted it would happen and was resigned to it. He just never imagined that they could go so far in ostracizing a fellow bishop the way they did him. His popularity with so many of the other bishops who sympathized with him made the traditionalists even more hostile, though to be fair, some of the old-fashioned bent were ever trying to understand and adjust to new ways. It was touching to see these men talking to David, trying hard to comprehend what he was attempting to accomplish and how he could square it with the theology they were all taught so many years ago. These men were just so conditioned to tradition that it was very difficult for them to accept such radical changes in their old age. They were kind men, even if they were somewhat rigid and unbending in their beliefs. They were not like those other traditionalists, who were really not religious people but just loved religion and looked upon themselves as the protectors of the sacred past. Angry, cruel people, they had minds like bear traps and the hearts of Pharisees. David instinctively feared these men, but he realized there was nothing he could do to protect himself against them.

David sensed that by the end of the conference he had acquired a host of new friends and admirers in addition to this small but powerful and well-connected clique of hostile reactionaries who would do anything to have him neutralized. He made up his mind not to let it bother him. That was God's business. He would try to get as much accomplished as possible before they caught up with him. Hopefully they would be too late.

Back home David rested and thought over all that had transpired at the conference. He was alternately sad and elated. He could see the enthusiasm of most of the bishops. They knew he was a prudent person and did not take his decisions lightly. They were more concerned about whether he could get away with it. If he did, that would give them hope. David appreciated their interest and their encouragement. The little coterie of hostile bishops worried him. It is never pleasant to experience the anger of your peers—especially when you know they are planning devious counter moves.

The weather was already beginning to change by the time the Bishops' Conference was over. Not long afterward the first snow fell, almost six inches. The garden in David's yard was completely covered. He had taken out the last of the vegetables, except for a few cabbages and Swiss chard which could survive a bit longer.

The house for the homeless was finished, and the people had moved in. David visited them frequently, bringing things for their enjoyment. They were like a family to him. A staff was formed from people of the local community to oversee the operation and organize its maintenance. Joshua did not stay with them as often as before; perhaps he felt they did not need him as much.

Other of David's projects continued bearing fruit. The schools were off to a good start operating under their new program. With the enhanced curriculum and prospects of varied religious instruction, children of other religions enrolled in the school, their numbers increasing little by little after word got around.

The community projects, like Bill O'Donnell's clinic, were progressing at different paces. The clinic was already under construction. A children's hostel was being constructed in another town. Plans were under way for senior citizen houses in a number of communities. A restaurant owned and operated by former prison inmates was set up under joint sponsorship of the four bishops (the Methodist bishop had since joined the team). The four of them tried to interest the Orthodox bishop, but he did not feel quite comfortable with the direction things were taking, though some of his priests were supportive through their people who were active in the community.

The four bishops had become even closer as they worked and planned together, which was an inspiration for the people to see. They even socialized at times with some of their laypeople. Almost everyone felt good about it.

Certain other denominations, however, were beginning to feel left out. Not having bishops of their own, they had no way of breaking into the bishops' circle.

When the bishops realized it, they tried to figure out ways to include the others. Their people naturally held positions on the various project boards, but that was a lot different than getting together socially.

The Jewish people were very much a part of the community programs, donating more of themselves and their resources to the enterprises than their numbers warranted. David had been invited to speak in their temples and synagogues on numerous occasions and was warmly received. He still attended his rabbi friend's synagogue on Friday nights when he was able. His ties to that congregation blossomed into such a beautiful relationship that the congregation's board invited David to speak at the dedication of a new hall they had just built. Out of appreciation of David's close friendship with the congregation, it was announced at the dedication that he was being named an honorary member of the congregation. The synagogue board had also worked out an agreement with David that any of their members who were personally drawn to follow Jesus would still be welcome in the synagogue as members in good standing. David's accepting membership in the synagogue was a way to express his belief that it was not incompatible with being a Christian. The episode made news headlines. Predictably, it also further irritated David's enemies, who by now were working up a dossier on all his "aberrations" from the norm of episcopal conduct.

The four bishops tried to be inclusive in other ways in their joint endeavors, but some smaller minority groups did not yet feel comfortable being involved, except on an individual basis. Invitations to Muslim groups were graciously declined.

In the meantime, the evangelical movement was making rapid advances throughout the diocese and among all the denominations. Ed Marcel arranged an appointment with David one day to discuss the possibility of introducing their understanding of Jesus into the schools and the religious education programs. David was reluctant to interfere, for these programs had always been independently operated, but the more they talked, the more convinced he was that a change was necessary in the way the faith was being taught to the young people. The young were not irreligious, in spite of their reputation, but they were particularly adept at distinguishing between what is real and what is phony. They had only too many examples of phony religion to turn them off. Ed's idea at taking religion courses out of the school curriculum and making it a living experience of Jesus' life and his thinking might make a difference in young people's feelings about their faith. It was worth a try—one, however, that would take planning, discussion, and acceptance by religious educators throughout the diocese. In the meantime, David could announce that Ed would be visiting the schools to talk to the students about Jesus and ask that the principals make generous time available. Based upon the response, they could then make a more realistic evaluation of the potential of this approach. Planning would take most of the winter and spring, and the program probably could not be scheduled much before late the next year.

Autumn passed by quickly. Before long everyone was busy preparing for Christmas. Advent was one of the most spiritually fruitful seasons of the year, and Christians should make more of it, David felt. Commercialism was destroying the preparation time for Christmas, and he wanted to counter the trend by introducing new customs and encouraging observance of the old ones. However, with everything else on full steam, he was unable to concretize his ideas. He had no choice but to postpone that project until the next year, with luck.

In this holiday season, David determined to make himself available to help out in whatever parish might be overburdened. On the morning of Christmas Eve he got an urgent phone call from a parish out in the mountains far from the city. The pastor, Father Ed Coleman, had been taken to the hospital during the night, and the people had no priest for Christmas Eve. Although David had the midnight Mass at the cathedral, he thought he would have time to offer Mass earlier in the evening at this parish.

On his way up into the mountains, passing through a village, the snow was falling heavily. To make matters worse, he discovered his car was running roughly. He had just passed a church on the main street when his car gave out. Not knowing much about these things, he didn't have the slightest idea what was wrong. It was already dark. The garages he had passed on the way were closed. David got out of the car, took his down jacket from the backseat, and zipped it up tight to protect him against the raw wind howling all around him. Walking back to the rectory he had just passed, he rang the doorbell once, then again. Finally a man in his fifties answered. It was the pastor, obviously annoyed at this stranger bothering him on such a busy night.

Not recognizing David—he looked nothing like a bishop—the priest asked him brusquely, "What do you want?"

David was taken aback. He certainly hadn't expected this merry greeting. He answered quietly, "My car just broke down and I'm at a total loss as to what I should do."

"Do I look like a mechanic? What are you coming here for? This isn't a garage. Don't you know it's Christmas Eve and we're busy getting ready for Christmas Mass? You had better find a mechanic somewhere. I can't help you."

"But—" David started to say as the door closed in his face. The thought flashed across his mind that he should have opened his coat so the priest could have seen his Roman collar and maybe recognize him.

David stepped off the porch, humbled, angry, wondering if that was the way this pastor treated his people. Again the rush of meanness in David wanted to punish the priest for his arrogance and un-Christlike behavior. But David fought his feelings and his pride. He went down the front walk and back toward his car.

On the way he saw two men approaching. As they drew closer, David wished them Merry Christmas. They returned the greeting, then one of them recognized David.

"Say, aren't you the bishop?" he asked, surprised.

"Yes, I am," David replied.

"My name is Tom McNamara, Bishop, and this is Jim Reilly. We're both deacons. We're on our way to the church to prepare for Mass this evening."

"What are you doing out on a night like this, Bishop?" Jim Reilly asked.

"I'm on my way to a church up in the mountains to offer Mass," David answered.

"You don't intend to walk up to that church, Bishop, do you?" Tom asked.

"No, I was driving, but my car broke down," David responded.

"Where is it? We'll take a look at it," Jim answered. "Tom's a mechanic, so you're in luck."

The three men walked up the street to the car. Telling David to get inside, the other two lifted up the hood and began diagnosing the problem.

"Try it now, Bishop," Tom yelled to David.

"Again," he yelled once more.

After trying a few things more, they called for him to give it another try. This time it worked.

David thanked them, shook hands, and took off.

The two men were delighted to have been able to help their bishop on Christmas Eve. They couldn't wait to tell the pastor.

When they walked into the rectory, all was quiet. They found the pastor sitting in front of the fireplace reading the schedule for the liturgy. The liturgy had high priority in the pastor's mind, and he liked to do everything with liturgical precision. It was his forte. After all, liturgy was the essence of religious worship.

"Come in, gentlemen," he said to the deacons as he pointed to the soft chairs on either side of him.

"Father," Tom said, "you can't imagine who we just bumped into."

"I don't have the slightest idea," the pastor answered tersely.

"The bishop," Jim replied.

"The bishop! What's he doing out on a night like this, and up this way?" the pastor asked, shocked.

"He was on his way to Father Coleman's parish," Tom answered. "On the way his car broke down, and we fixed it for him."

"His car broke down?" The priest seemed near panic. "How was he dressed?"

"He was wearing a ski jacket zipped up to his neck. I hardly recognized him until we got close, then I realized who it was," Tom said.

"Oh, my God," the pastor exclaimed.

"What's the matter, Father?" Tom asked. "You're as white as a sheet."

"I just kicked him out of here. He came looking for help for his car. I asked him if I looked like a mechanic and kicked him out. Oh, my God. How could I have been so stupid?"

The pastor's Christmas was ruined. He couldn't wait to call and apologize, although he realized that wouldn't help, because he knew David expected his priests to treat even strangers with respect and care. He had just failed, and miserably.

David continued on his way to the mountain village and offered Christmas Eve Mass for the little community there. They were grateful and thrilled to have the bishop in their parish for Christmas. David was happy to celebrate in such a simple setting. Those experiences were all too long past now that he was bishop and his official church was a Gothic cathedral with its elegant liturgies, huge congregations, and cast of hundreds.

The trip back home was peaceful and relaxing. There was a magic snow falling silently past antique village street lamps. People were warmly bundled as they walked along the streets of the quaint mountain villages, the crisp, new-fallen snow crunching under their feet with each step. It was almost ten o'clock when David arrived home, just in time to rest and drive to the cathedral for midnight Mass.

CHAPTER 13

MIDNIGHT MASS at Christmas was the one occasion that David allowed free expression to all the artistic splendor of the liturgy. During the rest of the year he felt it was important for the people to pray and sing together the praises and petitions to God. Christmas was just a time of joy, a chance to release all the pent-up longing and desire for the Savior the world needed so much. It was a feast of paradoxes. The Son of God stripping Himself of His divine attributes to become a creature totally dependent on others for his sustenance and survival, people of all types coming to worship him, the rich and the poor, the well connected and the disconnected, the castle dwellers and the homeless. They were all there sitting next to one another, brothers and sisters of the Son of God, strangers to each other.

The liturgy began with a procession to the stable off in a side chapel, where the figure of the infant Christ was placed in the manger. Then the Mass began. Out rang the *"Gloria in Excelsis Deo,"* that beautiful ancient hymn of the angels, this particular setting composed by Puccini when he was only sixteen, and expressing all the exuberance of a young teenager's love of life. It made one want to dance with joy.

As the Mass progressed, David read the Gospel story of the birth of the Savior, after which he began his sermon. He had been waiting all year for this occasion when he could deliver his first Christmas sermon as bishop, knowing that it would not be to just those in the pews and the aisles all around him, but to that whole vast unseen audience watching the ceremony on TV in their homes, all of them in varying degrees, Christians as well as the unchurched, still searching for that peace the Son of God came to give, hoping that by the grace of God they might find it this Christmas.

"My dear friends," David began, "what a beautiful Christmas this year, with the snow falling gently, covering the world like a soft blanket, transforming everything that was just a few hours ago so ordinary into a winter wonderland! As enjoyable as it is to walk through the snow to church on Christmas, we know that that is not the meaning of Christmas, nor are any of the other visible, sensible experiences the real essence of Christmas.

"Christmas is a hard reality. It is the answer to the world's longing from the beginning of time. The Jewish people to whom the infant Savior first appeared were chosen specially by God to give the world this night, when God sent His Son to show the way to peace and to give meaning to our lives, to tell us life does not end here.

"We all struggle to find a meaning to life, to find a sense of self-worth that will give value to our personal existence. Many never find that precious treasure and, in the emptiness of their meaningless lives, despair.

"We struggle for most of our lives to find what will give us happiness and peace. Little children, in their daily merry-go-round, flit from toy to toy, thinking that each successive one will make them happy. It does for a very brief time, then they discard it and find something else. It is an endless search. Older children no longer call their playthings toys, but they are still the objects of their search for meaning and fulfillment. They never satisfy.

"When we look at the infant in the manger, we see Him with nothing, not even a warm crib to sleep in. Even when He grew older, He still had nothing, yet He was perfectly happy, showing us by His own life that peace and fulfillment do not come from material possessions, but from the treasures within that God has given us.

"The treasure that we have within is the living presence of God, and His Son, who gives joy and peace and comfort to our hurting, hungry souls. My life was simple before I became a bishop. Now it is like a storm in the middle of a restless sea, with turmoil and crises and stress on every side. As frightening as events can become, and as ominous as the future is, I feel a peace I have never known before, a peace that doesn't come from anything material, or even from anything I have accomplished, but from deep within. When I stop in the cathedral to spend a few minutes in the presence of God, and know He is within me, there is a peace and a comfort that I can draw from nowhere else. I know then that my life is in God, and with God so close can anything else matter? Even knowing that hurtful things are in the offing does not destroy the peace. Knowing that He directs our life and understands our feeble attempts to be good and our weaknesses and, yes, our sins, and still loves us without condition and guides and protects us from permanent harm, that is peace.

"Each of you is a precious child of God. He created you special and gave you a work to do that is special. He also gives you all you need to do that work, and guides your life step by step so you can accomplish that special job. He will see to it, because He is your partner. Your lives may not be what you would like them to be. You may not have all that you would like to have, but God will make sure you will have what you need to do His work. In doing that work you will find your place in God's world and will find peace and joy in knowing that you and God are special to each other. Realizing that, you will one day understand that you need nothing more. It is the mystery of this night that has bonded us in a special way to God. Before we were just creatures; now we are His children, and Jesus' family, enjoying an intimacy with the Father that His Son has shared with us, an intimacy the world had never known before. That makes all the difference in the world and has changed our whole destiny. So tonight we just rejoice and are glad, and grateful. This is really the day the Lord has made. Let us enjoy it and be glad and enjoy as well the peace that flows from it."

David had noticed halfway through the sermon that a whole contingent of homeless people was sitting together on the side aisle watching and listening intently, feeling very much at home on this night when the Holy Family itself was homeless and unwanted.

The Mass ended in grand style with the congregation singing "Joy to the world, the Lord has come, let
heaven and earth rejoice"—as the people flowed out into
the snow-covered streets to begin their celebration of
Jesus' birth.

David spent Christmas with the homeless. He had
had presents bought for all the homeless in the various
shelters he had erected around the diocese. He had taken
seriously Joshua's injunction to care for them. He had
learned to depend heavily on their prayers, and that
made them feel as if there was a special purpose to their
existence.

Later in the afternoon David got a telephone call
from the pastor who had turned him out of his rectory.
He hadn't been able to sleep and couldn't wait to apologize to David. David was surprised; he had forgotten about the incident. All he said to the priest was,
"Father, you needn't apologize. It was a good experience for me to be treated the way ordinary people
are treated. It showed how sensitive we should be to
each one who comes to us, for fear that one day it may
be Christ, and, indeed, don't we teach that each one
is Christ? But don't worry, Father, I didn't take offense. Someday soon we will have to have dinner together. And I hope you have a blessed Christmas."
That was all he said. A few years ago David wouldn't
have been that understanding. He would have rammed
the lesson home strongly in a way the man wouldn't
have forgotten.

In the course of the day the four bishops exchanged
greetings and made it a point to get together that evening

at the Marxhausens' to celebrate the Lord's birthday. It was a joyous occasion. They all mixed well and were in rare spirits.

Late in the evening, when feeling quite relaxed, Don let slip a rather cryptic remark about how "one day soon we should all think about making the relationship between the four of us honest." The conversation stopped dead in its tracks. Everyone was stunned and didn't know what to say. Don turned red but hung in there and merely said, "Yes, let's think about it, because we've done everything we possibly could together but make it legal. I think it's time we took the big step." Everyone knew just what he was talking about but didn't dare express it. They just grinned, half in agreement. Then the conversation resumed, and the incident passed, for the time being.

A few days after Christmas, David called the Holy Father. He was glad to hear from him, though more memos were crossing his desk about David. The Pope wasn't concerned, because he knew David wasn't, but was glad to talk with him nonetheless.

"David, I have been hearing more and more about you lately. How are you handling the pressure?" the Pope asked, concerned, more for David than for the complications the issues raised.

"All right, Holy Father—John. I had an encounter with Archbishop O'Connell a while back. He's been tough. My chancellor feeds him all the information."

"Why don't you fire him? He's making it difficult for us all."

"John, I don't think it's the thing Jesus would do. He had His Judas, too, and kept him on. I feel God uses even Judases to get things done. I would rather trust God and leave the future up to Him."

"I admire you, David, but he's going to be your downfall," the Pope cautioned.

"I know, John, but I'm not afraid. With your help I can get done what I think has to be done in not too long a time. Even if you have to make a decision then, we will have accomplished what we wanted to accomplish and no one will be able to undo it."

"David, you're a tough one," the Pope replied with a chuckle. "I'll help you as much as I can, but remember, if the pressure here gets too great we are going to have to make some serious decisions."

"I know. John, I am going to have some interesting news for you in a short time. Christmas night the three Protestant bishops and myself met for a party. In the course of conversation, the question came up about us making our relationship honest. I think we are on the verge of something thrilling, and I would like you to think about it, because we are going to have to make a big decision. I think it is the chance of a lifetime."

"David," the Pope said with a long sigh, "Christmas has been very taxing. I'm really not up to another world-shaking decision. Can't we postpone this one for a while? I promise I'll think about it seriously. If we're not careful, you're going to get both of us kicked out of our jobs—me for insanity and you for, well, just for what you are."

"I just wanted to share it with you," David offered, "so when it happens, you'll be prepared."

"I appreciate it, David, but I'd appreciate it a lot more if you could just relax. You're not going to die tomorrow, you know. David, have a blessed Christmas and call back soon. You are still my dear son, though I'm happy I don't have many more like you."

"A blessed Christmas to you, Holy Father, and good health!"

Christmas week proved uneventful, and David kept in touch with those bishops he had met at the Bishops' Conference who supported what he was doing. It was a good time to speak to them because there was a lull in activities. They still showed interest in what David was doing, underscoring the fact that bishops, contrary to their reputation, were all not the hard-nosed conservatives many people think. David did not win over any converts who were willing to stick their necks out as he was, but they were at least open to change if there was the slightest possibility that it would work. That was support of a kind.

Toward the end of Christmas week, David went to one of the large state prisons in his diocese to spend some time with the inmates. This was his first visit. He was accompanied by a volunteer group attached to the diocese that counseled pre-parole inmates. Inside the prison they met with a group who had been assembling regularly for counseling in preparation for their leaving. The leader of the group was an inmate by the nickname of Bobo. He had been in prison for years with no possibility of parole but was determined to help the others who were leaving to make sure they could make a go of it when they got outside. He was like a father to the rest of the men, and could be tough on them when they refused to admit their own role in whatever had brought them to this place. David was impressed with the sincerity of these men. Flawed perhaps, some so seriously they could never survive in the world outside, but they were men who could be nonetheless saintly in their own unpolished way.

One of the most humorous fellows who picked up everyone else's spirits had been convicted of murder. All during the session David's attention was distracted continually as he kept analyzing this fellow. He could see the way the others cared for him. The younger inmates sat near him. Afterward David inquired about him and got a thorough biographical outline of his life in the prison. It had completely changed once he was inside. He had taken his high school equivalency exam and passed it, taken college courses, and received his degree in civil engineering. His cell was filled with oil paintings he had done while in prison, beautiful works of art that would stand against the best in any gallery. He had been saving whatever little money he made in the prison, and from the sale of his paintings, to send his little brother to college. David could see no justification for executing a young man with so much potential, a man who had made so much of his life. From that day, David was adamantly opposed to the death penalty as short-sighted and barbaric. Jesus demanded forgiveness and never losing hope in the mercy of God. The death penalty was the ultimate expression of despair of God's mercy and the human potential for goodness. It was unworthy of civilized society, to say nothing of Christian society. David wondered if those legislators who vote for the death penalty could do so if they knew the men and women whose lives they were destroying—or if they had to pull the switch themselves—because they were just as guilty before God, from whom they would one day be pleading for mercy.

David's visit to the women's prison was discouraging. He felt there was something about a woman that did not justify the same prison conditions as men, yet the crimes committed were similar to the men's, crimes of violence often associated with drugs. There was an apathy about so many of them that made him feel he wasn't reaching them. Then he reasoned that, perhaps, their own personal hurt was so great they were unable to trust anymore or open up to even the most gentle and caring, for fear of further hurt or rejection.

When he left the women's prison he wondered if a different solution couldn't be worked out for women. He thought he would like to try an experiment if his people could work out something with the courts or the legislature.

14

AROUND the middle of January, a committee of bishops met to discuss the future needs of the Church in American dioceses. David was a member of that committee. One of the most critical issues they were facing was the severe shortage of priests. The shortage had become so critical that already over ten percent of the parishes in the country had no priests. In another fifteen years eighty to ninety percent of the parishes would be seriously short of priests, or they would have priests in their late sixties and seventies. What should be done to prevent this disaster? Import priests from Poland or Czechoslovakia or Africa? That was the solution some advocated. The archbishop, who was also on the committee, was all for bringing in priests from Poland or Lithuania.

"I am opposed to that solution," David said. "They may be saintly men, but they are totally unprepared for the kind of life we have in our country, where there are so many Protestants. We have through the years learned to appreciate the positive contributions of our Protestant brothers and sisters, and how their religions complement our own. To Eastern Europeans who have never had to work and associate with Protestants the way we have, it would be difficult for them to understand the development of our relationship with non-Catholics.

"I strongly disagree," the archbishop protested calmly. "They are confessors for the faith, they have suffered much, and we would be blessed by their presence here. They would be an inspiration to our people."

Twenty years ago, the archbishop would never have suggested such a thing. The Church was more conservative then and the last thing anyone wanted was an influx of even more old-fashioned conservatives who had no understanding of our way of life. Now, however, the Church was threatened by what the Europeans called a materialistic, secular, liberal priesthood in America. The archbishop and his kind agreed. So a large contingent of conservative priests was no longer seen as undesirable. They would be a great asset.

Most of the bishops disagreed. One old bishop, the one who befriended David at the Bishops' Conference and kept asking him questions, spoke up frankly: "We have had them before. It never worked out. They have serious problems with the language and often have a mentality that severely clashes with our people's whole culture. Rather than being inspired by them, our people are turned off and look upon them as strange. They represent a mentality we outgrew forty years ago, and no one wants to go back to it."

"What do you mean?" Archbishop O'Connell asked rather sharply.

"I mean, very simply, they come from another world. Forty years ago the Protestants were our enemies. Our theology, like theirs, was apologetic, defensive, argumentative. Then came the World Wars. Our boys, Protestant, Catholics, Jews, fought side by side, protected each other, died for each other, worshiped at each other's services when there was only one chaplain, began to see the goodness in each other for the first time. They saw things in each other's religion that were lacking in their own. They came home with a wholly new, healthy view of religion and even of God, who was not as petty as they used to think. Having learned that, they can't unlearn it. When they came home from the wars, they were godparents for each other's kids. They married each other's sisters. They learned to look upon others as God's children and not enemies. Is that bad?

"And that is where we are as Americans. It is the product of a profound learning experience. To go back to where we were is unhealthy. And that is what some would have us do. We have learned that our religions complement each other, make up for each other's short-comings. Together we have a lot to offer. Separated we lose something. We have come a long way.

"Those behind the iron curtain have had different experiences. There the message was: We are under attack. Don't budge, don't give an inch. The enemy is lying in wait to destroy us. Hold fast to what you learned and don't compromise. That represents a church under siege. That kind of mentality may produce martyrs, but it does not lead to enlightened thinking or bold advances in theology. It stunts any real growth. To bring priests like that over here would not be fair to them or to our own people. They could never understand the giant steps we have taken with our Protestant brothers and sisters. For those reasons, I would be opposed to it."

Coming from an old man who had a reputation for

taking the hard line, that carried weight. David just listened, applying everything to his own situation. He did have a shortage of priests. In another fifteen years, many more of his parishes would be without priests. He remembered what Joshua said about God giving more vocations than the Church was willing to recognize. He shared some of these ideas with the committee. They listened politely, but his suggestions, as usual of late, were outside the accepted parameters, so they barely heard him. If they would open their minds to the Spirit of God and consider the long-term good of the Church, they could stand firm and fight for something that affects so deeply the life of their people. Ultimately they would win out. Having been conditioned to be obedient, however, such talk and line of reasoning was forbidden. Like well-trained children they obeyed.

David came home from the meeting feeling guilty that he had not done more to solve the problem in his own diocese. His people needed priests, not to be there day and night, but to preach the word of God and make God's presence felt in the community. There were many communities that rarely saw a priest. It was his responsibility to provide them with priests.

No sooner was he home than he got Dick Franey on the phone. "Dick, I have to see you. Can you come over tomorrow night for supper?"

"Oh, another one of those deals?" Dick said jokingly.

"Yes, in fact I think we'll have a doubleheader," David replied.

"How did the bishops' meeting go?" Dick asked.

"The way you would expect it would. If you were a member of the Politburo, you would know what things you could talk about and what things you couldn't talk about. You could write the minutes of the meeting before you got there," David answered.

"David, do I sense a trace of cynicism?" Dick questioned.

"No, I'm not cynical. I accept their positions. There are some who are really open and could do wonders if they didn't feel intimidated by the presence of a handful of traditionalists. They're self-righteous, so much like the Pharisees in every way. They're long on law and rigid observance, but they're merciless. They'd cut their own kids off if they had any who wouldn't toe the line. They have never learned what true religion really is. As Jesus said, 'It is not sacrifice I desire, but mercy.' Those people have never learned what mercy is, either, and care little for the needs of the people. They say the Church is not a democracy. We know it's not a democracy, but when people clamor it's not a democratic movement, it's a desperate cry of human need. These men coldly turn a deaf ear and feel not the least pangs of conscience. That's what Jesus was talking about when He said it was mercy He wanted."

"You're really wound up, aren't you?" Dick remarked.

"I suppose, but I do get sick of their pompous pious prattle. I suspect it will always be that way. That's why I am the way I am. Rather than waste time talking, I'd rather do what I think should be done and let the chips fall where they may. What can they do to me but censure me, or send me someplace where I can do no harm? By then it's too late. So I'll see you tomorrow night, and we'll plan our next move."

"If I keep hanging around with you, I'll never be made bishop," Dick said jokingly. "Good night, David."

"Good night, Dick."

The next day at the chancery, the schedule was routine. David checked with the director of social services on his projects. The director was pleasantly surprised at the progress of the new directions. They made a lot more sense and united the diocese in a way he never thought possible. The diocese was now one big family; people from all over were involved and getting to know one another—even priests they had never heard of before. Christian life was becoming fun. "I have to admit," the director said, "I did have my misgivings in the beginning. Now everything is working like a charm, and there's a wholly different spirit among the people."

"That's what I was aiming at, but it was hard to get the idea across in the beginning. I guess it was all too new," David said.

David left early in the afternoon. He wanted to track Joshua down. Other than bumping into him at the farm on one visit, he hadn't seen him since harvest time. He hoped he might be there today. They had a lot of catching up to do.

Joshua was at the farm. David invited him to the house so they could talk. He consented, and they drove off.

"Joshua," David started, "many things have happened since I saw you last, some of them good, some disturbing. I need to talk about them and sift everything in my mind, so I don't act precipitously and do something imprudent."

"What could be so earth-shattering that you have to get upset over it?" Joshua asked softly.

"I don't have your calmness, Joshua, so things do get to me," David replied. "Like the problem of the shortage of priests. I've been doing a lot of thinking about that, and we just had a meeting to discuss that very problem. The bishops have no way to resolve the issue. The only way to do it is by making some hard decisions. That's the way I see it."

"What do you have in mind?" Joshua asked.

"We already have over twenty parishes without priests. In a few years that will be tripled. I have a responsibility, whether the Vatican agrees or not, to provide priests for my people. I can't create them out of thin air. Do you have any suggestions?"

"David, why do you get so upset?" Joshua repeated. "The answer is simple. What did Saint Paul advise? 'Pick men of tried and proven virtue.' Every parish has them. Find them and call them. They have already been chosen and have been waiting, without even realizing it.

"That's all you're going to tell me?" David questioned, baffled.

"What more can I say?" Joshua responded. "The answer is simple. God is giving the calling but the Church is rejecting those whom God has called. If you pick those people you will have more than enough priests for each community. They can still work at their jobs and do the Lord's work besides. In time maybe the people will support them."

"But those men are married. It's forbidden," David objected.

"David, all I am doing is showing you the ones God has called. I am not going to answer objections. If you want to be responsive to God, you have the answer. If you want to follow everyone else, then I can't help you."

"What about the Vatican?" David again objected.

"I know the Pope is a holy man and would like to do what is right. But his advisers are politicians and listen to voices other than God's. Talk to your friend. He has helped you before. You can trust him. He is Peter."

By this time they were at David's house. It didn't take long to prepare supper. The two men talked while David cooked and Joshua helped.

During supper they continued talking. David was beginning to realize that if he was going to be true to his vision of that first night, he would be sealing his doom. He was beginning to realize that it was becoming impossible to follow the laws as they existed and still be a shepherd true to Jesus. He had not had misgivings before, but now he could see the noose tightening. He could not help but be apprehensive.

"Joshua, I know you know what's happening. I am only a human. It is difficult to be alone in doing God's work. I have never lacked confidence, and I know I have a reputation for being determined—some may call it stubborn. But at times I feel the loneliness of being a pariah. It is not easy, and I wonder if I could be wrong. Who is there to talk to when you are on a road like this? Everyone is afraid. They listen, and you see the sympathy in their eyes, but they are afraid to express their feelings for fear of compromising themselves. I have never been one to buck the system. I was always so very careful. That's why they made me bishop. I am not used to being alone like this. Am I right or am I wrong?"

Joshua listened. Then, slowly, calmly, looking at David, he said, "David, how do you think Jesus felt? The very ones who should have introduced Him to God's people were His bitterest enemies. You are in no different a position. When you ask yourself, 'What would Jesus do?' the answer is simple, but to follow is a way of the Cross. Church leaders are no different than anyone else. They may have good intentions, but they are not God. They may have the good of the Church at heart, but they, like others, rarely ask themselves, 'What would Jesus do?' So they run the Church and people's lives on expediency, not on what is good for the people or what God wants. Jesus never used the Scribes' and Pharisees' laws as the basis for his decisions, though they were the teaching authority, the magisterium, of His day. He asked Himself, like the prophets before him, 'What is my Father's will?' The answer was simple, but it led inevitably to the Cross. The answer for you, David, is also simple. Following it will lead to the Cross, but always remember: After the Cross is the Resurrection. My Father has called you special, David, to renew the Church. To do this you cannot be afraid, even though you feel alone. You will accomplish this work. You must trust in Him and not fall prey to doubts, and you must not look back. Above all, you must not give up. Look ahead and be brave. My Father will always be by your side."

What more could David say after that? The supper conversation continued in a lighter vein, and afterward David invited Joshua to stay for the evening. He agreed.

As David tossed in bed that night, he realized more than ever that he wasn't prepared for living this way. He had always been part of the team. To be a maverick, an oddball, was not in his nature, and it made him uncomfortable. There was no longer any support, no one to reassure him when he was treading dangerous ground. His only hope was in not allowing himself to waver, and not allowing doubts to cloud his vision. He realized that though he looked strong and sure of himself to others, inside he weighed every move and every decision he made against his inner sense of what God expected of him. Somehow it always used to seem so clear.

15

THE dark, cloudy days of winter passed by slowly. Ed Marcel had accomplished wonders throughout the diocese by preaching to a people who were hungry for Christ. He had been invited to a number of schools to talk about Jesus. Even the children were touched and afterward asked their teachers why religion couldn't be taught like that all the time.

It was well into summer of the following year that David's three bishop friends requested an appointment with him. They had something very important to discuss. David asked if they wouldn't rather come over to his house where the atmosphere would be a little more congenial. No, this was official business, and they didn't want to get sidetracked by the temptation to socialize.

They came to his office one morning, the beginning of a beautiful summer day.

Marxhausen was the first in the door. David was there to meet them. "What a beautiful day! Either God is trying to tell us something, or the devil is doing his damnedest to distract us. We almost changed our minds about coming and took the day off instead," Don said as he walked inside the air-conditioned hall.

"No, it's just that some damn fools don't know when to relax and enjoy themselves," David said jokingly.

David ushered them into his private room and left word he was not to be disturbed.

"Gentlemen, a little something to drink?" David asked.

"Coffee will be good enough for me," Allan said.

"The same for me," Don agreed; Jim seconded the choice.

David poured the coffee from the large pot on the counter and served it. The men then got down to serious business.

"David," Allan said pensively, "the three of us have been doing a lot of thinking and talking lately. It is rare that four bishops get along as well as we do. And it is not just ourselves. Our people for the most part support our cooperation with one another and seem to enjoy the fact that for all practical purposes our churches have become one. We have discussed doctrinal differences. I have been brought up on Catholic theology. I even went to a Roman seminary. In talking to the others we have found a substantial theological agreement among ourselves, and I am convinced it is pretty much compatible with what you believe. Knowing your own relationship with the Pope and how you understand his position gave us a good insight into the reality and limitations of his role. We have no problem with that. We do accept the fact that he is Peter, and Peter is very much a part of Jesus' heritage. What I am leading up to, David, is this. We have decided that we think it would be good and pleasing to God if we were to team up and become one, working together as one flock as Jesus would have it if He were here."

David couldn't believe what he was hearing. "Are you saying what I think you are saying?" he asked, amazed.

"Yes," Don said. "We have discussed it thoroughly together, and thought about it individually. The conclusion is always the same. What do you think?"

"I'm speechless. I don't know what to say," David responded.

"Well, you better not be speechless too long," Jim said, "or we may lose our nerve and change our minds."

"Really, I am thrilled," David finally said, still not quite believing what he had heard. "This is a first," he continued. "Do you realize the implications of what you have done? In one whole vast territory there will be for the first time just one flock and only one Shepherd, Christ himself, with we four stooges as His helpers. We'll have a million and one details to work out before we can pull it off, but I'm sure the Pope will be thrilled, and will help us get through the red tape."

The four men discussed the matter for almost two hours, exploring various possible difficulties. Jim Dorsey anticipated one: his own ordination as bishop being accepted neither by Episcopalians nor Roman Catholics. He requested that David reconsecrate him conditionally just to sidestep any potential objections.

It was lunchtime when they finished their meeting. David insisted they eat with him before they leave. Nothing was discussed at the luncheon other than world news, small talk, and light topics. Their own news,

which was to become national headlines, was not discussed. The staff was itching to know what was transpiring between these four good friends who were
meeting so frequently. They knew David was not the
type to idly socialize. There had to be something important, very important, to explain why he was spending so
much time with these men.

After lunch the visitors left. David went across the
street to the cathedral and knelt at the prie-dieu before
the Blessed Sacrament. In a few moments he was
wrapped in prayer. Why were all these things happening
in his life? Maybe Joshua was right. Maybe God had
called him for an extraordinary mission. He certainly
never dreamed when he became bishop that his life
would take this turn. He had always tried to be ordinary
in everything. Now nothing was ordinary. It seemed so
unreal. If he had planned to accomplish the things
that were happening, he wouldn't have known where
to start. Now things just happened, apparently disconnected events all falling into place like parts of a
carefully designed machine. He was thrilled God was
using him so powerfully, even though he knew he was
in no way deserving. But, then, maybe that's the way
God works.

David was aware how most people thought. When
good things happen in our lives we think they are rewards for good things we have done. But God doesn't
work that way, he was seeing that now more clearly than
ever. Even at our best we are frightfully deficient. We
fall so often and are so hurtful of others and so unfor-
giving ourselves. We use so little of what God gives us
for His good or to help others. We think of Him so

rarely. We are so little aware of His presence in our lives or of the many good things He does for us each day. We sin continually, not in big ways, perhaps, but in a thousand little ways. Even the best of us are crippled spiritually. So, when good things happen and God uses us to accomplish His great works in the world, it is not for anything we have done, but because He understands our humanness and in His own greatness of spirit chooses to share His intimacy with us. Through our weakness He touches the lives of others.

Rather than feeling proud when he finished praying, David felt humble, realizing that what was happening was not his work, but God's work. He just happened to be there when God needed someone willing to cooperate. It was nonetheless fun to watch the magic of God's goodness.

That night David called the Pope. He was not in his usual good humor but was quite concerned about the developing complications of David's projects and unorthodox decisions. It wasn't so much what David was doing—that was logical enough—but the reactions of important clerics who worshiped traditions and practices that no longer worked that were creating problems which were rapidly destroying the Church's credibility in a world that was less patient with a backward clergy who were like fossils of another age. Jesus excoriated the priests of His day for their irrelevant rules and their insensitivity to the anguish in people's lives. Church leaders had become similarly notorious, for refusing to lift archaic laws that destroy people. They drive more people away from the Church by their callousness than theologians with far-out ideas whom they condemn for damaging people's faith, the Pope knew. But they are in charge, so their power must be carefully weighed.

"David," the Pope began, "the temperature over here is getting quite warm lately. Your decisions are an annoyance to not a few people."

"It hasn't been exactly a picnic here either, John," David replied calmly. "I realized the implications of what we were doing, but I never anticipated the viciousness of religious people. I am convinced that people's attachment to religious forms is not theological but the obsessive behavior of rigid personalities. One can see it in the hateful way they treat their own grown-up children who try to exercise their freedom in matters where their parents disagree. It closely borders on child abuse and psychological kidnapping. The more I see these people operate, the more convinced I am that we cannot allow these people to influence the Church, much less run it."

"I agree with you, David. That is why I have been willing to give you all the permissions you need to work toward a model that we can hold up to the world as what the Church could be like. I am sure, however, this was not why you called."

"Holy Father, I have had the most inspiring meeting today. Remember my three Protestant bishop friends? They came to visit me with a proposal. As you know, we have been working together on a number of projects, in addition to our joint religious services. I have been preaching in their churches regularly. The three of them suggested that we form one flock. They are sure most of their people will follow them."

"David," the Pope said, his voice showing obvious delight with the news, "I think that is wonderful. We have a matter like that under consideration here. An Episcopal bishop is becoming Catholic. It is a shame, however, that our people here don't know what to do with him. I don't want that to happen in your case, so we'll work this one out ourselves. What is it they would like to do?"

"Well, they want me to accept them as partners or fellow bishops in one church, so we could have one flock," David replied. "They are, all three of them, saintly men, very closely attuned to the spirit of God. I have been impressed with the genuineness of their spirituality."

In the brief silence that followed, David could sense the Holy Father's indecision, but he continued anyway.

"Holy Father—John, why can't they just continue working with me the way we have been, without making a big thing of it?"

"David, you always see things as so simple."

"But it *is* simple. What could be simpler than four bishops with four different constituencies deciding to work as one family in Christ? They merge to form one flock and collaborate as a team."

"What about the Methodist bishop? Is he one of the four?" the Pope asked.

"Yes, but he himself already anticipated the problem and asked if I would consecrate him conditionally to obviate any objection."

"Have they met with our theologians to see if their beliefs are compatible?"

"I have talked to them for over three hours, Holy Father, and I find nothing objectionable. But I'll have our theologians meet with them to fulfill the requirements.

"This is the chance of a lifetime to have one flock in an entire area. It should provide a beautiful example of what ecumenism can accomplish with a little imagination," David said.

"I can see that, David, and it makes good sense, but I am afraid we will have a difficult time with some people over here, as well as with some of your own."

"Why do they even have to know about it? Why can't you just give me permission and I'll send over to you whatever paperwork is required? You can process it through someone you can trust over there."

"David, you never give up, do you?"

"John, once it is accomplished, we will have a model no one can retract. It will point the way for others. I'm willing to take the blame for it but at least it would have been done."

"All right, David, I'll have the papers sent over to you. Have the three bishops fill them out and send them back here as soon as possible. I'll do what I can to help. I have to admit, it seems truly the work of God, if it didn't appear so easy."

"Maybe that's the best proof that it is the work of God, Holy Father, the fact that He has made it work so easily," David answered.

"David, try to take a rest for a while. No more bombshells. My cautious nature can't take much more shock."

"I'll try, Holy Father, but there are so many problems to be solved and so little time," David answered respectfully.

David thanked the Pope again for being so accommodating and hung up jubilant. He waited until the next day to call the three bishops and tell them the good news. They were beside themselves and asked about the next steps that had to be taken. David described the procedure. In their joy they started discussing plans for a celebration. He had to remind them it would take a good while before the process could be finalized.

After the phone conversation, David centered his attention on other matters. The projects in the various communities required ongoing attention. He wanted more than anything else for those projects to succeed so the communities could work their way to being self-sufficient in responding to local needs. The social services director met with David to report progress. There were fourteen projects either in planning stages or under construction. The clinic in Bill O'Donnell's parish was almost complete; it would open by late fall. Three senior citizen housing projects were already approved. Each would have its own clinic so residents could have readily available medical care.

The school venture was progressing far better than David had anticipated. Industry was duly impressed with the quality of the training after they brought a number of students into their factories for summer jobs. More schools had implemented the program in the past year and more industries, some from outside the area, had signed up after hearing of the satisfaction of the companies already involved. The result was a public relations bonanza for the industries. Attendance at the schools doubled. Ministers and religion teachers from each of the denominations registered to teach their own children. There were also comparative religion courses that attracted students of varied religious backgrounds. Since the schools were no longer Catholic schools but

186   JOSEPH F. GIRZONE

fully integrated ecumenical public schools, they could be eligible for substantial tax consideration and aid of various kinds.

David was ecstatic over the success of the programs and was proud when bishops from many other dioceses contacted him for information. Articles in national magazines praised the operations and provided visibility throughout the country. The schools performed a valuable service for the vast numbers of students who were highly talented but not academically oriented or did not have high IQs (a seriously defective measure of ability anyway, David realized). In another few months the first graduates would be hired by the sponsoring industries, fulfilling the promise of immediate employment after high school. A high percentage were minority students who would have had employment difficulty otherwise.

When other large industries that did not have branches or factories in David's diocese saw how their competitors were benefiting from the programs, they contacted the chancery asking if they could become part of the system. This broadened the program even more, offering to the students a wider range of training and employment opportunities. Many industries were suffering serious shortages of skilled labor due to the effects of the severe drop in the birth rate, which was threatening the future of their operations, internationally and otherwise.

While the schools were thriving, however, not all was rosy on some other fronts. The diocese still suffered from a lack of priests. The problem gnawed at David and gave him no rest. He was determined to solve it no matter what it took: he felt he had a responsibility before God to provide shepherds for his flock. Joshua made him realize even more painfully that the hierarchy was not listening to God, insisting instead on preserving archaic forms and practices that no longer answered the needs of God's people. Indeed, it seemed only too clear that Church leaders were more concerned about laws than they were about people, just as in Jesus' day.

Another problem troubling David was the discontent among a handful of extreme right-wing priests and lay-people. They rarely if ever talked to David personally but attacked him from behind in the dark, spreading rumors about him, reporting him to friends in high places, bringing tape recorders to his speeches and jotting down notes to use out of context. They cared little for truth. They needed ammunition—like the Pharisees—to convict him. They hardly cared how they got it. This they would send to national right-wing magazines and newspapers, then forward copies of the spurious articles to the Vatican in an attempt to discredit David.

There was no way he could confront these people, because they were so devious. Rarely employing a positive approach themselves in trying to solve problems, they tried to frustrate David's attempts to answer the crying needs of the people. They were still his people and David cared and was concerned for them, but they placed themselves so out of range it was impossible for him to reach them. David knew his chancellor was in daily contact with these people and from behind the scenes orchestrated many of their moves. The archbishop himself was only too willing to give ear to their reports, promising to bring them to higher authorities.

That explained why David was beginning to get phone calls from the Vatican and from the papal pronuncio, the Vatican's representative to the country. Those calls were never pleasant. The accusations that prompted them were never accurate, and the officials grilled David on his version of the case. He was fortunate in having all his sermons and speeches recorded; minutes of every meeting he spoke at were transcribed by secretaries. He was honest in answering all the questions asked by the officials, although he didn't reveal matters that were between himself and the Pope, of course.

Indeed, the Pope himself was beginning to feel pressure from these people. He had had so much trouble with the Vatican bureaucracy during his first few years in office that he fast realized that his own staff was the greatest obstacle to his carrying out his lifelong dreams and ambitions. That was why he was so willing to go along with David. He knew David and trusted him. He could see in David a chance to finally implement, if vicariously, his own ideas for reform and show to the world through a limited experiment that change could work, could be a powerful vehicle for the renewal of Christ's message in a fast-changing world.

Trusting David's intelligence and prudence and even more so his uncanny efficiency in accomplishing whatever he set his mind to, the Pope was delighted to do through David what he found impossible himself because of insurmountable resistance.

One day, Jim Mohr, Ed Marcel, and Dick Franey

asked if they could see David at his home. David agreed, and they came out after supper one night. Ed Marcel was the most outspoken of the group; he started the conversation.

"David," Ed began, "the three of us are really concerned about something that's been going on for a long time now. Your secretaries, and practically the whole chancery staff, know about it. They have become protective of you lately, appreciating all that you have done for the diocese. But no one seems to know quite what to do about it."

"What is it, Ed?" David asked.

"Well, it's about Charles," Ed ventured after a pause. "Ever since you have been in office, he has made it a personal mission to undermine everything you do. He's in constant contact with the archbishop and reports everything to him. We're afraid that with all that's going on, and all the good things that are taking place, he's going to ruin it all."

Dick then added his remarks. "He's right, David. The archbishop's canon lawyer and I are good friends. We studied in Rome together. He told me everything that Charles has told the archbishop, and a number of bishops and cardinals are already contacting their friends in the Vatican to have you removed."

"I appreciate your telling me all this—I've known from the first day what he was doing. It worries me sometimes, but then I think of Christ. He had His Judas and never did anything about it. I have tried so hard to do what I think Jesus would do, and I keep coming up with the same thought: 'He has a place in God's plan and I shouldn't interfere.' So I'm not too terribly concerned. I feel God is going to protect our work, which I know is basically His work."

"David, I admire your trust," Jim Mohr said. "I sensed you knew about it, but couldn't believe you could be so charitable to him knowing that he was undermining every good thing you were trying to accomplish."

"I do appreciate your concern, gentlemen, but I have assurances which I will share with you someday. I am certain that no matter what he does, there is no way he will be able to frustrate what we are trying to do. Let yourselves be at peace. Shall we have some refreshments?"

"Sounds like a good idea," Dick said.

After a while the three men left, feeling better after talking to David. They admired his trust in God, but they couldn't help wondering about his ability to put up with a Judas in his household.

Still, though David did have a deep trust in God, he was beginning to feel the strain from the constant covert opposition. No one enjoys being misunderstood. No one enjoys having a Judas. It was painful to not defend himself. He knew each priest and layperson involved in the plot against him and when he met them he treated them with kindness, without the least sign of bitterness or hostility. He refused to be petty and stood tall in his friends' eyes as a result. This bothered his enemies even more. Did he hold them in such contempt that he considered them unworthy of even a response?

Yet as strong as David was there were times when he fell victim to deep discouragement. He had dreamed of being bishop for a long time. After only a short while as bishop, he felt his future could only be bleak. At times like this he would spend hours trying to pray but unable. It seemed even God had distanced himself.

And then, in the darkest hours, Joshua would always appear, either in the garden, or knocking at the door looking for something for the homeless. They would then spend hours talking, Joshua reassuring David that he had not done wrong, that everything that he had done was in faithful response to his Father's guidance and that he should have no fears for the future. Just trust. Always trust.

"Joshua," David would end by saying, "it is easy for you to say that. You are strong and seem immovable as a rock. I am a mere human and don't feel confident all the time. I have misgivings. There is no one to talk to who understands these things but you. If it were not for you, I don't know what I would do. Alone, I would never have had the courage to undergo what I have the past few years."

"David," Joshua told him, "just remember, my Father's work is not yet done. This is only a small part of it. Trust Him, even when things look dark and bleak. Always trust."

"Thanks, friend," David responded. "You are my strength, even though I don't even know you. It is strange. At times I think I do, but then I pull back, not daring to think. But I am so grateful for all you have done. I know terrible times are ahead, and I am afraid. I hope you will be with me then."

"I will always be with you, David," Joshua answered reassuringly. "Never fear. You are not alone. We will always be with you."

Joshua left shortly after, David driving him to the

farmhouse, taking with him packages for the homeless. Bill, David's houseguest, often spent what little money he had buying things for Joshua's homeless, and whenever Joshua came to the house Bill would give them to him. These things were also included among the items Joshua brought with him.

16

No DAY was normal or routine for David anymore. Each day might start out normal, but what took place during its course was unpredictable. There was so much change and upheaval in the Church, so much unrest and discontent over the insensitive way clergy dominated Church life, that one group or another was always trying to make its voice heard. David, as hard as he might try, was unable to please everyone. Radical women's rights groups complained he wasn't doing enough for women in the Church, hadn't changed the language of the liturgy to suit them, or didn't change references to God from "Father" to "Mother." Handicapped groups complained he wasn't sensitive enough to their very real needs. A handful of Arab Catholics were upset because they felt he showed favoritism to the Jews by going to the synagogue so often. Some Jewish groups were upset because he once made a remark that he thought out of fairness to all the different religions, Jerusalem should be an international city or an independent city-state, where everyone could feel free to visit their sacred shrines and worship God without political bickering. With all that David was trying to do to change things, some people were still unhappy that he wasn't doing enough to address their particular concern. So each day saw one group or another demanding an audience to talk with him.

One group he did have real sympathy for was a group of laypeople who called themselves "'Just Average Catholics." They were upset because they felt the Church was dominated by intellectuals and that church services were designed for the elite.

"Bishop," their spokeswoman, Betty Ann, said to David, "most of us don't understand what is going on in church. The liturgy was designed by intellectuals and it is too complicated for us ordinary people. We have problems, we hurt, we need to be comforted and supported. To come to church and watch a cold, formal, intellectual worship service, and hear a sermon we can't understand, leaves us cold and undernourished, and we walk out of church still hungry. We would like to have someone talk to us about the Bible and explain to us confusing things about religion and help us understand what it's all about. Protestants stop off at our houses to talk about the Bible. They visit us when someone is hurting or when someone dies. Our Church doesn't seem to care at times like these. We don't feel we are part of a family, even though that was one of the things important to Jesus, to develop a sense of family among his followers. I think our Church is too big and because it is so big, it doesn't care for little people anymore."

David listened, jotting down notes every now and then. "Betty Ann," he finally said, "I couldn't agree with you more. I know you are right and I can't understand how we got where we are. What you are all concerned about is perhaps the most important issue facing the Church today, the alienation that so many of our people feel. Our liturgy, which was designed by theologians, was not tailored to the needs of ordinary people, so it is difficult for many people to find comfort in it. What do you think we can do about it?"

Another member of the group responded, "That's hard to say, Bishop. We know you have tried hard to make our religion more caring."

"What would you like to see done?" David asked, trying to prod them into offering suggestions.

"Do we have to go to Mass every Sunday?" a man asked. "Couldn't we meet in smaller groups in our neighborhoods and have a simpler liturgy, and Eucharist, and talk to one another about the Bible and our faith, about problems in our personal lives, so we could help one another?"

Another added, "That's right. When you have five or six hundred people herded into each Mass on strict schedule and herded out to avoid parking problems, it doesn't make sense. We are supposed to be a family, and we don't even know each other's names. Some parishes have ten thousand members. People come to church but are not being fed. Why do you think people are going to evangelical churches? Not because they provide spiritual depth, but because they provide a feeling of companionship that people need, that they have a right to as Christians. Those new priests who are going around talking about Jesus—they are good. Why can't we have that kind of sharing on Sunday mornings, so we could all get to know Jesus better?"

"I have to admit you are right," David said. "What we can do about it is going to be a problem. We teach that the Church is the mystical body of Christ and that we all have an important role to play in helping one another, yet so few feel they are needed or wanted. Let me think about it for a few weeks and see if we can't come up with something that makes sense."

After the group left, David made notes to make sure he would follow up on the discussion. It was a matter that had concerned him for a long time, and he had not known what to do about it. The Church's size and durability were a powerful mark of the authenticity of its origin in Christ, but its sheer numbers made it unwieldy and demanding of tight controls, which gave it an image of coldness and aloofness which was offensive to many. David realized that many educated and highly successful Catholics who were used to more attentive treatment in society were finding life in the Church difficult. Overworked clergy were often looked upon as socially crude and uncouth when compared to the openness and respect for others' opinions that were needed for healthy social living.

Now the ordinary people were expressing dissatisfaction, feeling that they didn't belong. Later on in the day David discussed the matter with Joshua. As usual, his insights were precise and to the point. "David, people are lonely and hurting. They need to find God in one another. The Breaking of Bread was intended to gather God's children into intimate sharing as family. That isn't happening. The people who spoke with you this morning are expressing that need. Jesus spent His life teaching people they are family and that if they want to be close to God, they must find Him in one another, not just in ritual."

"But how do you solve the problem when you have so many people?" David questioned Joshua.

"David," Joshua replied, "let the people meet in smaller groups with their own leaders. God has called many more as priests than are now recognized. Some may be married. That has never been an obstacle to God's call, so choose persons 'of tried and proven virtue.' They have already passed the test. They are stable and spiritual. They will be a credit and not a liability."

"What about the Eucharist on Sunday?" David asked.

"Jesus offered His Body and Blood as a gift, not a forced obligation on scheduled demand. Be open to change, David, if you want to respond to the needs of God's children. The law was made for them, not they for the law. If you respond to those whom God has called, you will have enough priests to share the Eucharist. There are varying ways to doing things. 'Don't put new wine in old wineskins; put new wine in new wineskins,' as Jesus said."

Joshua wouldn't spell out the details, but he further opened David's mind to possibilities and to the realization that old forms are not sacred, especially when people are starving.

Distressed over the two critical problems in his diocese—the severe shortage of priests and the clamoring of people for a simpler way to God and for sharing faith with family—David spent much of his unoccupied time praying and groping for a solution. It was almost two weeks later that he decided to call Rome and discuss matters with the Pope.

"These issues," David told his friend, "are so serious

they must be faced. Almost sixty-five percent of our people are just ordinary people. They are good people who are looking for more to their religion than just going to church on Sunday. They love the Eucharist, but they want more. They need to meet and get to know one another. They want to share the experiences of their faith and some of the problems and troubles in their lives. They really are longing to find one another. We have no vehicle for them to meet and spend time together as family. Our parishes are too big, some with as many as ten or fifteen thousand people. With such numbers intimacy is impossible."

"What are you trying to tell me, David?" the Pope asked.

"I would like to break up our parish structure," David replied, "and let the people meet in smaller groups in their neighborhoods. There they could have a simpler liturgy centered around the Eucharist and an expanded sharing of Scripture, in which they can all take active part. People would have the option of going to the main parish church for liturgy or take part in their neighborhood liturgies. In order to do this we are going to need more priests. In every one of our parishes there are men whom everyone admires and respects as exemplary Christians, married men with families, many of them professionals. They would make wonderful priests and would be much less of a liability than many we have now. I would also like to call back some of those who have left. We really need them."

The Pope listened intently. He was impressed with the way David was handling changes so far. And while he wished that he would go more slowly, he also realized

he did not have much time left. The pressure was clos-
ing in on both of them, and if they were to have an
irreversible model, it had to be in place very soon.

"David," the Pope responded with a trace of sad-
ness, "I am afraid this is going to be the critical issue
that will set off the explosion. I have thought about this
time and time again and have been unable to resolve the
problem to everyone's satisfaction. I know we have to do
something. I am willing to let you go ahead with men of
your choosing, even if they are married. I cannot see my
way yet with women. Theologically I am not opposed to
it, but I'm just afraid."

"How about ordaining a few of them as deacons?"
David asked the Pope.

"As deacons, I could allow that. At least it would be
a start," the Pope answered. After a pause he continued.
"David, I am afraid this may be the last. Not a few of
your colleagues have very well placed friends over here
who have been exerting a pressure the likes of which I
have never seen before. Even some of my friends are
becoming concerned because of the viciousness of their
tactics. They won't rest until they destroy you, David,
and even me, if they don't get their way. I have to admit,
the Pharisees are still very much alive. I'll try to hold out
as long as I can but character assassination is the forte
of these people. For them truth and goodness are not
goals to cherish, but obstacles to be demolished. I am
afraid for you, David. At least we have accomplished a
far-reaching goal that will be a beacon for all to see in
the dark night we are passing through. I will do what I
can from here to preserve it intact."

"I am grateful, John, more grateful than I could

express. I never dreamed we would have been able to go as far as we have and in so short a time. I realize we had to move quickly. The surprising thing is that it is the people who are grateful and supportive, and our own who are being difficult, together with a small band of those who always oppose progress of any sort. Their problem is more psychological than theological. Change undermines their stability and causes panic. That is the only way you can explain how these otherwise good people could become so vicious."

"David, don't let this trouble you. They can't do any real damage. I still want you to feel free to call me. And remember, whatever happens, I will always hold you in high esteem."

"Thank you, Holy Father. Your friendship has been a powerful support. I have another friend here who has been good support. He is a strange man who has an uncanny sense of spiritual things. He knows of the need for change. His name is Joshua. I can't tell you all the times he has pointed a simple, clear way through complicated issues. I wish you could meet him someday. He lives frequently with homeless people. I think he is very close to God. I've seen him do things nothing less than miraculous. I've wondered about him more than once. He has an amazing sense of Scripture and of Jesus' mind. He makes everything seem so simple."

"You are fortunate, David, to have a friend like that. I suppose we are both fortunate. He has been a help to both of us," the Pope said, leaving David wondering.

"John," David said in ending, "I'll begin working on these matters and let you know how everything is working out. I'm confident of the future, though I realize there is going to be trouble. I hope you don't have to feel the brunt of it."

"Don't be concerned. I've survived many plots in my lifetime. I'll survive this one. I have a feeling I'll be around for a long time. It is you I am concerned about."

17

NOT LONG after his conversation with the Pope, David had another session with Dick Franey. Dick never dreamed he would find himself in the position he was in. He was a good canon lawyer and prided himself on being calm, judicious, and a highly respected canonist. His admiration for David and his loyalty to him, however, had placed him in legal positions detrimental to his standing in higher ecclesiastical circles. As David's canonist, he would absorb the blame for many of David's stands on issues. His reputation would rise and fall with David's.

Dick realized this, but he was so impressed with David's courage that he couldn't refuse to help him, even if it did affect his own future in the Church. David had told the Pope on a number of occasions how much help Dick had been, and how sharp he was as a canonist. He also told him that he was concerned about what might happen to him if there was trouble. The Pope listened and only said that David should not worry.

David's session with Dick covered a range of subjects in rapid succession: the restructuring of parish life, the calling of married men to be priests, the request for women to exercise more active roles in their newly developing small communities. One decision in particular that Dick opposed was the ordaining of women to the diaconate. Dick felt this would be the last straw and believed that David should avoid it. However, David felt the issue had to be faced; it was a matter of justice and a shameful denial of human rights. A precedent was needed, and, once ordained, the power could not be revoked. But Dick would not back down on this one. He was adamant in his opposition.

David's next move was to call together key people from various neighborhoods to discuss revamping parishes and allowing people optional worship services on Sundays. He spelled out in exact detail what he had in mind and asked if they would discuss these ideas among themselves and report back to him in a reasonable time.

Almost all of David's agenda was in place. What remained was to tie loose ends together and watch it all work. The three Protestant bishops had met with a team of theologians and canon lawyers. Their theology was acceptable and their quick course in Church law brought them up to date as far as the everyday running of the Church was concerned. Most of their respective parishes remained loyal to them and followed their lead. The three bishops met with their pastors and their people over the next few months to discuss theological differences and work out problems. Finally the date was set for all the flocks to become one. What better date than the feast of Pentecost?

The celebration was a glorious event. Every church throughout the area simultaneously celebrated the triumphal answer to Jesus' last prayer: "Father, that they may all be one even as you, Father, are in me and I in

204 JOSEPH F. GIRZONE

you; I pray that they may be one in us, that the world may believe that you sent me." There was no triumph of one over another. There was no compromising either. Each brought the rich heritage of their own understanding of Jesus' message; they would all share it from now on. There was one flock guided by four bishops of equal standing with Christ alone as Shepherd. If there was a sense of triumph, it was a triumph for Jesus Himself. The Episcopal cathedral and the Roman Catholic cathedral timed these celebrations so that all four bishops could be present at each church, both cathedrals now being co-cathedrals of equal status at which the bishops would take turns officiating.

Not all, however, would be perfect joy. Some disgruntled people from each of the churches refused to go along. The three bishops worked out an arrangement whereby they could keep some churches where they could worship as before and remain separated. Some Catholics were angry at this "travesty and mockery of true religion." It was for them the ultimate triumph of Protestantism that they were now overrun by Protestants and had to accept these bishops, especially at their children's confirmation.

Joshua attended. David wanted him to sit in a place of honor, but Joshua was content to sit in the back of the church and enjoy the flock celebrating the coming together of their families. Joshua's face glowed with happiness, and an inner joy radiated from his eyes and his smile. He was like a child at Christmas. He was just content to be there enjoying the people's celebration, sharing his Father's joy. He needed no place of honor, no audience. It made no difference that people were bumping into him or that a crippled lady needed his seat or that no one had the slightest idea who he was or what his interest was in being there.

At both cathedrals the bishops took turns saying a few words, each expressing their joy at being able to answer the plea of Christ for unity and the fact that this was truly an historic moment for God's people. After the ceremonies, the bishops and their wives had a party. David tried in vain to find Joshua and felt bad he couldn't be there celebrating with them. After all, it was his vision that made possible this momentous miracle.

Each day now was reaping new surprises. The modified school program was graduating its apprentices. The industries were more than pleased with the quality of the students who were accepted for employment in technical positions in the factories. There was now talk of expanding the programs starting at the elementary level. Music, art, and languages were considered for students gifted in those areas, beginning at fifth grade and continuing through high school. Chinese, Japanese, and Russian were to be among the choice of languages. By high school graduation, the students would have had eight years of those languages and should be able to speak fluently as well as write the language of their choice.

Although David was gratified by the progress made in most of the schools which incorporated the program, in outlying areas its performance was disappointing. Adjustments had to be made and experiments tried to bring expertise to those schools so their children could benefit from those highly practical courses.

On other fronts, David was receiving daily reports.

Bill O'Donnell's clinic was now functioning. It was the pride of the community. Teenage drop-in centers, halfway houses, day-care centers, industry-sponsored training programs, a diocese-wide program to build low-cost housing for young couples, and health-related facilities— these were all in varying stages of development. Church support of the communities would insure the ultimate success of all these projects.

David's involvement was minimal. His director of social services was working full-time with the vast network of local communities and the planning and implementation of these projects. His initial reaction to David changed in the course of time from apathy and distrust to enthusiastic support, as he began to see the vast, far-reaching potential of all these programs. To see people of every possible background working together toward common goals was exciting, something not often seen on so wide a scale. He, for one, was beginning to recognize in David the uncanny genius that was not always apparent on the surface.

Ed Marcel's regular reports more than justified David's decision to allow him to continue working as a priest. His preaching of Jesus drew wider and wider audiences, more than half of them evangelicals and fundamentalists attracted by the richness and depth of his understanding of Jesus' personality and teaching. Many of the priests on Ed's team were reluctant in the beginning and had to be pried loose from their parishes, but they were more than rewarded when they saw how people responded to their new ministry. Some, for the first time, truly felt they were apostles who preached the word of God to a hungry world.

David, although he continued to preach at the cathedral every Sunday, was spending less and less time at the chancery. He spent most of his time visiting the farflung communities of the diocese. The people felt blessed to have four bishops so intimately involved in the life of their communities. A bishop was no longer a person they saw on rare occasion for confirmations but an integral part of their ordinary life as Christians working in the community. It tied everyone together in a closely knit family. The fact that the diocese was generous in sharing its financial resources with each community also helped. People responded accordingly when the diocese asked for help in turn.

David's greatest pride, the result of his newfound respect for industry, was his success at encouraging industries to sponsor employment programs in inner-city neighborhoods. Buses were sent to pick up people and bring them to training centers. The outcome of this extraordinary effort was full-time employment of practically all the employable people in the inner city. Some chose to accept jobs with companies in other cities. Everyone who wanted to work was given a chance, and in time, with steady income and the good salaries many of the people were making, and with help from special diocesan funds, many were able to purchase their own homes.

All that remained in David's plan was reorganizing parish worship and the calling of people to the priesthood. David had ceased accepting volunteers for the seminary. From real-life experience he could see how inadequate and dangerous such a procedure could be. The real motives that brought men to the priesthood surfaced only after ordination, in the life-style they adopted and in the way they treated people. Real motives could be too easily hidden even during the long years of seminary training. David wasn't taking any chances. "Men of tried and proven virtue, married only once" was Saint Paul's qualification for bishops. David and pastors of every parish could easily identify such persons and call them for the priesthood.

After conferring with the other bishops and calling a meeting of all the pastors, David was ready to introduce the program. From each of the three hundred parishes, the pastors selected at least four men, working men with families, most married, some widowed, a good number of them professional men. At first they were just asked to meet with David. A good number agreed. At the meeting, David explained his new vision of parish life. Most thought it was brilliant. A few were upset and told David they wanted no part of it. The plan was that the men would study theology and Scripture and canon law and, after their training period, would be ordained as priests in their parishes. They would only be expected to work part-time and could still keep their jobs, though they could spend as much time at priestly work as the Spirit prompted. Since most of the men were approximately fifteen to twenty years from retirement, the parish would pay a minimum stipend now, to be increased at retirement.

The response was overwhelmingly positive. Of the thousand men who came to David's meeting, almost six hundred were willing to enroll. David was anxious to get going as soon as possible before the opposition had time to organize. He knew they would have a pitched battle on their hands before long, and it would be hateful. He was determined to have a number of the college graduates who had already taken theology enter accelerated courses so they could be ordained without too much delay. The program also allowed David to bring back a number of priests who had married and were still willing to resume their calling. All this had to be done expeditiously. The Pope agreed to tie up and delay any restraining orders from Vatican congregations until David had a chance to get the program off the ground. Their strategy would probably include ordaining some men before their training was complete; they would take the last year of Scripture and theology after ordination.

The initiating of the program was directly related to the reorganization of the parishes. The committee David had requested to meet with him had been thorough in their homework. They had practical ideas about alternatives to Mass every Sunday. Most wanted to keep Mass a part of Sunday worship since the Eucharist was so important, but they suggested the Scripture time be expanded so people could discuss Scripture at greater depth. Many felt there should be more time to get acquainted and socialize. It was the general feeling that if this was the route the bishop was taking, there would be a need for more priests and deacons. Could the bishop see his way clear to ordaining women as priests?

David took all their suggestions to heart and with a small group of advisers tried to faithfully respond to what the people felt was important. It was decided they would buy or rent already existing facilities in each neighborhood. In some places they would have to build new facilities. Would the people be willing to carry the added burden? Their answer was positive.

Although David, out of deference to the Pope's insistence, would not ordain women as priests, he felt he could open the door by ordaining a few women as deacons. That in itself was revolutionary; he fully expected it would stir up a tempest. But it was a move in the right direction toward opening the door for further changes.

As for the places to meet, David left that up to the people in each neighborhood. They had to make all the decisions necessary. In due time he would be ready to provide deacons and, he hoped, priests from each neighborhood. The program could start as soon as the new priests and deacons were ordained.

When Charles Mayberry realized the extent of David's reforms, he was beside himself. He had been keeping the archbishop informed of everything David did, but this latest was monstrous and unthinkable. He told the archbishop immediately of David's plans, hoping they could be thwarted. The archbishop, at first, couldn't believe it was true. He knew David had it in him to make real changes in the structure of things, but he never believed he would go as far as to oppose Vatican directives and laws to ordain married men as priests and women as deacons.

He called David immediately to see if it was true. David admitted it was and that he had no intention of changing his mind. The archbishop also grilled him about the reported merging of churches and the three Protestant bishops being accepted as equals in the administration of the diocese. Did it happen with Rome's approval? If so, why wasn't he informed?

The phone call went poorly. David saw no reason to have a meeting over the matters discussed. The archbishop hung up, determined to do all that he could to obstruct every one of David's moves. He contacted other bishops and cardinals who were close friends and informed them of what was happening. They in turn called David or wrote him scathing letters accusing him of rebellion against authority, of tearing the Church apart, of gross violations of sacred traditions, and of trying to foment a schism within the Church.

David had already decided not to get drawn into a debate. He just listened and was polite and thanked them for their concern and interest and asked for their prayers. Realizing they were getting nowhere with him, the archbishop and his cohorts decided to contact their friends at the Vatican.

Still, this would all take time. David knew that.

It was at this point the Pope was of greatest help. David had called him informing him of everything that was happening. The Pope stalled the opposition's maneuvers in Rome, delaying the issuing of the cease and desist order and his permission to proceed with the investigation of David until David had already ordained his first group of married priests. These stalling tactics were the same strategy used by contrary cardinals to frustrate the Pope's efforts to make changes in the beginning of his pontificate. Now he found those very same tactics very effective, and used them with great skill and timing.

A positive note in this increasingly troubled scenario was the unexpected support David received from his fellow bishops, both in his own country and from around the world. He had had the courage to initiate precedents that could alter the course not just of the Catholic Church but of Christianity itself. It would be difficult if not impossible to reverse them, particularly if the Pope could be encouraged to let things continue if only as an experiment. What the whole body of bishops had not the courage nor wisdom to accomplish, David alone had the boldness to execute. His fellow bishops expressed their admiration for his courage and foresight and wisdom in gathering together all the churches into one flock.

David's three colleagues were supportive in their own quiet way. David insisted they stay in the background and not get involved. He knew he could be dispensed with, but they had an important role to play in the future no matter what happened to him. It was important that they not be considered to have colluded with him. Their places among the combined flock were important.

Events moved rapidly from then on. David was bombarded with incessant communications from bishops and Church officials in various places, as well as from Vatican congregations. Telephones rang endlessly. Newspaper and radio and TV reporters hounded him for interviews. His whole life had dramatically changed. He was no longer able to do his work as shepherd of souls. He was now the object of intense curiosity.

In the midst of all the stress, though, he tried to maintain an inner calmness and peace in order to do his day-to-day work. He still took care to assure the continued progress of all his programs and projects. He brought the other three bishops closer into his confidence so they would be aware of all the intimate details of his initiatives in case they had to assume responsibility.

During all this excitement, Charles Mayberry alternated between elation and anxiety; elation over the fact that the Vatican had decided to take a stand against David and anxiety that David, in his shrewd cunning, might still outfox the opposition and pull off all the radical changes. Charles realized he himself could do nothing more. Like Judas, who had turned his Master in, he now had serious misgivings. The whole chancery staff, who had been merely sympathetic to David originally, now idolized him. They had turned against Charles. Even his secretaries refused to work for him. The archbishop, who now had no further use for him, never bothered to return his phone calls. He was despised by everyone. Realizing that it was useless to show up for work, he asked David for a transfer. David, decently enough, picked out one of the best parishes in the diocese for him, in keeping with his status as chancellor, and appointed him pastor. However, in no time, after the parishioners realized what he had done to the bishop they all loved, they refused to accept him as their pastor. He tried to stay on the job as long as he could, but people would have nothing to do with him, even after David's entreaties to be kind to him. Eventually he requested a leave of absence. He asked the archbishop if he could work for him, but the archbishop wasn't interested.

Finally, Charles went to stay with some friends who owned a national conservative newspaper that backed Charles in his efforts to undermine David. Now that they smelled blood, they were even more vicious in their articles about David, through which they hoped to force a showdown with the Vatican. Many Vatican officials had a reputation for being sympathetic to the views expressed in the newspaper. As disreputable as it really was, it had found a new way to thrive on the business of character assassination of good and decent people.

18

MONTHS went by. Nothing happened. The news media were curious, the archbishop was furious, the people were anxious. The suspense was unbearable. Why had drastic action not been taken? Why were there no cease and desist orders demanding that David stop the flagrant violations of Church law and accepted traditions? Only David and the three bishops seemed unperturbed through it all. David's plans continued unobstructed and on schedule, everything working like a well-tuned engine. His telephone conversations with the Pope were less frequent, but to the point. The Pope remained faithful to his word. He had on his desk the request from the prefects of the congregations to investigate David but would wait until David was ready to be investigated.

"Have you ordained your married people yet, David?" the Pope asked. That was his chief concern.

"Yes, John, our first group has just been ordained. The second group will be ready in another two months," David replied.

It was for this group's ordination the Pope had been waiting patiently. That would give David over three hundred more priests. They would have to finish their

theology the next year, but at least they would be ordained and functioning.

"Are the three bishops secure in their new positions,
David?" the Pope asked, concerned.

"I have brought them all into my confidence and told
them everything," David answered. "They are a bit ner-
vous. They have never experienced anything quite like
this on such a scale, but I think they will be all right."

"You know, David, once the investigation starts, it is
not going to be pleasant. There is no way I can let you
get away with everything, and hard decisions are going
to be forced upon me," the Holy Father said, half apologetically.

"I know, John, and I am ready for it. I've done about
all I can do here. The model is in place. That's the
important thing. No matter what the outcome, I am
ready," David responded. "My friend Joshua has been a
great comfort."

"You're a brave man, David," the Pope said, "and a
good shepherd. I don't want you to worry. I'll do what I
can from here."

"I appreciate that, John, and I am grateful. Everything is ready here. Pray for me and give me your blessing," David said before saying good-bye.

The stage was now set for the drama to unfold.

The second wave of ordinations took place. Only a
few days later the order from the Vatican congregation
came for David to cease and desist from ordaining married men. It was too late. There were already over six
hundred new priests. David noticed a loophole in the
order. The order was addressed to him personally, which

meant that if anything would happen to him, the order could not apply to his successor.

Besides the cease and desist order, investigators were sent from the Vatican in the persons of two bishops. They were to go through the chancery and interrogate everyone from David to the cook. David had wisely kept everything to himself. Their best source of information would have been Charles, but he was nowhere to be found.

The two investigators, however, were not what one would expect, indicating that the Pope had had a hand in the appointment. They were gentlemanly and courteous and showed a sense of fairness and objectivity in their conduct of the investigation. They talked to David for hours. To make it less embarrassing for him, they asked if he wouldn't be more comfortable at his own home during their discussions, and so they interviewed him there.

The Pope had made the three new bishops exempt from the interrogations, for which they were grateful. Although they approved of what David did, they understandably preferred not to become embroiled in controversy so early in their new careers. David had by this time introduced the three bishops to the Pope, and they had already had a number of conversations with him about the significant issues. They promised their support.

It was at this point that David's genius for being a spiritual leader shined its brightest. The news media had received information about the Vatican investigation. When the news broke, the people were angry, hurt, even furious with the Vatican. Unfortunately, the Pope was their target, and David could say nothing about the real truth, although in his televised talks at the cathedral each week he encouraged the people to be understanding of the Pope and to remain loyal to him as the successor of Peter. In public he appeared strong and undaunted, but underneath he was shaken by the severity and swiftness of the changing tide of events.

All the goodwill that David had cultivated by his Christlike attitudes was being undone by the Vatican officials in one simple gesture. An individual theologian or bishop who departs from traditional practices or views does damage only to the outer garments of the church: the insensitive, uncaring actions of some Vatican officials, all too much like those of totalitarian governments condemned by the Church, inflict massive havoc on the people's faith—the Church's "soul."

Even though David had been expecting all of this and knew in his heart most of his goals were secured, he began to experience a frightful unhappiness. He had never been exposed to anything like this. At times he was angry. At other times he was depressed and discouraged. He loved the Church; to see it rent and torn and tortured like this hurt him deeply. To think that something he did was the occasion of this tearing at the Church's innards was even more painful. In happier moments he realized that in the long term, the Church would be the better for the struggle, and with God's guidance much more advanced in its response to people's real needs and pains. Nonetheless, the depression continued to eat at him.

Joshua met with him frequently and tried to comfort him. Their conversations proved priceless to David.

"David, you have followed where my Father has been leading you at each step. Why do you trouble yourself about what is happening? It is working just the way God planned it," Joshua said to him one day as they walked across the field near David's house.

"It is easy for you to say that," David replied. "You don't have to take the abuse as I am now."

Joshua laughed. "David, it is all in your perception. Nothing has even happened. Your plans have been fulfilled. You have been reassured by Peter that he will support you. Where is your trust? My Father isn't even done with you yet. You have just begun. Don't lose heart now."

"Just begun?" David said in astonishment. "Here I am finished, and you say I have just begun. I don't see where you get your logic, friend, or your information for that matter."

"David," Joshua said, trying to reassure him, "you like everything clearly spelled out in every detail, the way you do things. God doesn't work that way. People couldn't stand knowing what is going to happen tomorrow. No one would get out of bed. God's care is so tender He expects people to trust Him and have confidence that no matter how bleak things look, He will work wonders for their ultimate good."

" 'Ultimate,' that's the hook," David answered cynically. "The ultimate is when God takes us home. The rest here on earth is trouble."

Joshua laughed again. "David, this isn't like you. You have kept your fears locked inside for too long. Now you are having a hard time. What are you afraid of?"

"I don't know. I guess of being disgraced by what they could do."

"No one can hurt us but ourselves. Your work as a shepherd is faultless. It has been God's work, and you have done it well. Do you think my Father is so insensitive and ungrateful that He will let you be disgraced? Tested and tried a little more, perhaps, as He prepares you for another work. But not disgraced, nor destroyed. So have heart, David. He protects you and watches over you more than you think. He needs you."

"Another job?" David questioned. "You think He's still interested?"

"Hear me, David, this job isn't done yet. The best is yet to come, believe me."

"I believe, Joshua. I am just weary from driving so hard and not knowing what the future holds, but I believe and I trust."

After their walk and long talk, David drove Joshua back to the farm. It had expanded considerably since the first days, and both David and Joshua were proud of it. The motley group David first met in the abandoned barn had been transformed into a beautiful family, from being concerned only about themselves to really caring for one another.

The investigation lasted for a number of weeks, though information had been gathered since the first day David took office as bishop. The Pope kept a discreet eye on every step of the process through one of his own trusted advisers, who gave him a daily progress report. When it was finished and the final documented account was given to the Pope with recommendations, the Pope spent the whole night reading it, analyzing every word of it. He could see firsthand how information filtering into the best Vatican minds could be twisted by the seriously flawed characters providing the "facts." The Pope knew each step that David had taken, every minute change he instituted in his diocese. He now could see just what happens to facts as they are "faithfully" reported to Vatican congregations. His first reaction was to send the report back and have the investigation done over, saying that he knew differently, but what would it have accomplished? It would further prolong David's agony. The recommendations were what the Pope was really interested in.

They were many. First, David, being guilty of serious incompetence in administering his diocese, should be immediately relieved of his position. Second, he should be severely censured and penalized for his blatant violations of canon law, long-accepted customs, and traditions of the Catholic Church. He should be required to make an extended retreat at a monastery known for its rigorous penitential discipline.

Nothing was said in the report about any of the good work David had performed during the short time he was bishop. That was obviously not one of their concerns. They were concerned merely about the well-ordered observance of ecclesiastical laws and customs.

While the Pope was still considering the document and all its implications, a serious blunder was made by someone on the congregation's staff. A copy of the document was sent to the publisher of *The Vagabond,* the religious newspaper that had been reporting on David. Thinking they had a scoop, they ignorantly published excerpts and details of the document before it was officially approved by the Pope. The whole country knew about it. Not knowing what to believe, David at first felt betrayed by the Pope and hurt, until Joshua told him not to believe it, and that he should contact John and talk to him. This David did. The Pope was furious and assured David that he had not accepted the document officially yet, and that he should still trust him and not worry. He also promised to make up to him for the public humiliation he had suffered.

As soon as he finished talking with David, the Pope summoned to his office the cardinal prefect of the congregation and the staff who handled the case. He told them that he was not going to let this pass, that their report was a perfect example of poorly researched and shoddy workmanship, and that he felt personally betrayed by what they had done in leaking the document to such a disreputable newspaper. They had obviously shown their true loyalties. He told them that he knew more real facts about the case than their report revealed. He now saw how faulty they were in gathering objective data and offering unbiased recommendations on such extremely important issues. He told them they had personally done him a terrible injustice by the way they handled the matter. He would make a determination concerning that in the near future. In the meantime, he would make his own independent decision on this matter, which he guaranteed would be significantly different from their report and its recommendations. Handing the report back to the cardinal prefect, manifesting his rejection of the document, he dismissed them.

The staff walked out of the Pope's office humbled,

ashamed, and badly shaken. They had never experienced anything like this in all their years of service to the Church. Their future in the Vatican was in serious jeopardy. The cardinal prefect met with the staff immediately to find out who had leaked the document. No one would own up to it. It took a while, but the cardinal, through his own contacts, finally discovered who had sent the document. He called the priest into his office and castigated him for having given the congregation a black eye before the whole world, not to mention seriously embarrassing the Pope, and ordered him to request an audience with the Holy Father and apologize to him personally for what he had done.

CHAPTER 19

The *Vagabond,* which broke the Vatican report, had to retract its article on David Campbell as false and without foundation. Reputable newspapers that took the chance and reprinted *The Vagabond*'s story regretted it. Some had the decency to call and apologize to David.

The Pope issued his own statement in the case, a highly unusual move. To save face for the decent members of the cardinal's staff, he quoted some of their valid findings, then gave his own adjudication of the case.

"There were many noble and beautiful things attempted in the diocese during Bishop David Campbell's few years as bishop," the Pope wrote in his statement, "which should not go unnoticed or unappreciated. These changes will have profound effect on the course of not only his diocese, but of the Church itself. The Church at large has a glowing example of ecumenism at its best, with one flock and one shepherd.

"Some of the changes, while seemingly far advanced for our time, have already proved beneficial and highly practical. These changes, although not strictly in conformity with previous and present-day customs within the Catholic Church, have shown potential for resolving critical issues, so they will continue in that diocese until we decide otherwise. In appreciation for the prophetic and courageous work that Bishop Campbell has performed in his diocese, we are hereby naming him archbishop and appointing him to a diocese to be named in the future where he will have the time and freedom to perform for us the invaluable task of setting down on paper his vision of the Church in the future. To assure the continuation of the programs that Bishop Campbell has inaugurated, we are hereby appointing as bishop to succeed him Father Richard Franey, who will work with the other bishops in that diocese on an experimental team, answerable to myself personally."

The letter was sent to the papal pronuncio for immediate release to the press. A copy was forwarded to David and another to Archbishop O'Connell.

The letter was like an atomic bomb, unleashing a light and heat that no one expected. The pronuncio was noncommittal. The archbishop was so distraught when he realized that all his scheming had backfired that he locked himself in his room and was uncommunicative for days, refusing to talk to staff, the press, or other bishops. He was a defeated man and felt, more than anyone else, betrayed and rejected.

The hierarchy was stunned. The Pope, through David, had set the Church on a wholly different course, and on not just one matter but a whole range of issues that could dramatically alter the course of Christian life far into the future.

David received the letter with a resigned spirit. He was happy with the sensitive way the Pope had handled an extremely delicate situation. He never dreamed it would be resolved as cleanly as it was. He did not feel let down. He was sad to see his work ending, knowing he was unable to carry it to the heights he would have liked. He probably would never get another chance. While the news was not announced publicly, David's correspondence from Rome also included the location of his new diocese, a large tract of land covering an area of over twenty thousand square miles . . . of desert sands and impossible mountains in the western part of the country. There were some people living in the new diocese, but not many; certainly not many Catholics. A demographer might predict a population boom in that area for sometime in the future, but certainly not during David's lifetime.

Surprisingly, David was not discouraged. After his last conversation with Joshua, he felt the ability to trust, and he did. God came through. The Holy Spirit was still guiding the Church, cleverly. David broke the news to his houseguest, who had been growing frail of late. The poor man cried like a baby. David had been like a father to him, literally picking him off the streets and giving him a home. David offered to take him with him, but Bill said he was too weak to make the long journey. David told Don Marxhausen about him and said, jokingly referring to the fact that Bill was Lutheran. "He's one of yours—you'll have to take care of him from now on."

"Still dumping on me, just the way you started," Don retorted in good humor. He agreed to take Bill into his house if he was willing to come.

David had to make provisions for his house. It was a large house, with plenty of land around it, far enough into the country to be away from noise and distractions. It was a good place for people to come to think and pray. He decided to turn it into a house of prayer for trained men and women who could teach people how to pray and benefit from the rich mystical traditions of the Church that are the key to a more intimate relationship with God. The house would be big enough to accommodate at least twelve people overnight. A permanent ecumenical prayer community of five or six could staff it. In time it would have to be expanded. David talked one of his wealthy friends into endowing the house of prayer, thus assuring its survival.

David picked up Joshua at the farm right after he received his letter from Rome and took him out to dinner, at a fancy restaurant this time. Joshua ribbed him about it but went anyway. They both had a good time.

"Joshua, I'm surprised it went as well as it did. I know I'm not getting a prize in my new assignment, but the Pope requesting me to write down my ideas for a reorganizing of the Church is something I could spend years working at and praying over. And in my new place, I'll certainly have the time to do it—not much else but time. Maybe that's why he is sending me out to the desert, like John the Baptizer, and Moses and the others, to be prepared for God's work."

"Now maybe you will trust," Joshua responded. "It is fun when you work for God, David. You are just learning that. Most people think that if they get too close to God, it will take all the fun out of their life. What they don't realize is that God created them to have fun, and finding Him is the beginning of the greatest adventure of their life, filled with more fun and happiness than they could imagine."

"I can see it now," David agreed, "but it is hard to believe it when you seem on the brink of disaster. Joshua, I'll miss you when I leave. You have helped me more than anyone else in my life."

"You don't think you are getting rid of me that easily, do you?" Joshua retorted. "Your work is just beginning, which means mine is not yet done, so don't be in too much of a hurry with your good-byes."

"I don't know what you know," David replied, "and I know now not to ask, but if I should see you again, maybe you can help me with my research. You were never at a loss for ideas, and I can't remember you ever being wrong. It must be great to never be wrong."

"You are being wise, David. We just learn to steer a more careful, steady course when we get older, and learn not to make mistakes," Joshua answered.

David called Dick Franey to congratulate him. Dick was more shocked than happy about the whole thing. He felt sad for David but was glad the Pope kept his word. He promised to be faithful to the changes they had both engineered and that he would try to be tough when the pressure came on. He asked David if he wanted a going-away party. David was not keen on self-congratulating parties, but when Dick and the other two bishops made him realize it was not really *his* party but the *people's* party, the chance they needed to express their own feelings, David gave in.

The chancery staff prepared for a party the likes of

which had not been seen in years. Everyone took part. It was held in the civic stadium. There was food and simple pageants. The celebration started in the morning and lasted all day. People came from everywhere: towns, villages, farms, cities, factories, shipyards, schools, hospitals, prisons. . . . It was a rare outpouring of love and veneration, particularly for a cleric. Dick Franey had insisted on this grand celebration for David; for himself he wanted only a simple ordination ceremony, with David as presiding bishop.

It was almost two months later when David departed for his new diocese. The four bishops accompanied him to the airport. All had tears in their eyes when he boarded the plane.

It was a long and lonely flight for David. He was leaving his whole life behind—everything he treasured—to go out into the desert. God still hasn't changed His ways, he thought with grim humor. He still has a thing for deserts. Moses, Elias, the prophets, John the Baptizer, and now David, leaving his life's greatest accomplishment to go off into a wilderness. For what? To write, and only God knows for what else.

David's plane landed at a little airport on the edge of the desert. A small delegation of local priests and people met him at the airport. They were happy to see him, but their timid looks betrayed their uncertainty about whether or not he would be happy to see them. David put his bag down and warmly embraced each one of them, thanking them for being so kind as to meet him and expressing his happiness at being their new bishop. He said he hoped he wouldn't be a disappointment to them.

The ride back to the house where David was to stay

was long and hot. The car was not air-conditioned. David asked them about their families, about their work, where they lived, and how many people there were in the diocese. The diocese had a total population of only fifteen or twenty thousand people, with only three thousand Catholics. As it was a new diocese, it had just twelve priests.

The house where David was to stay was an old Spanish adobe ranch house that had been abandoned for years because it was so far away from everything. It was the nicest building in the diocese. The people were so proud to show their bishop his new residence. Most of them lived in hogans scattered throughout the desert. There was a well attached to David's house, which the people said had never gone dry in over four hundred years, so if David wanted to have a garden, there was plenty of water for irrigation. The people would be honored if they could cultivate it for him.

David couldn't help it, but his heart sank when he saw the place. It was so different from his old childhood home, with all its comforts and modern conveniences. David never could stand hot weather. Here there were no conveniences and only hot weather, searing heat all day and into the night. He was immediately gripped with a sense of panic, which took all his years of discipline to conceal.

Inside the house the rooms were furnished simply. The welcoming committee was proud to tell David they had made the rugs with their own hands especially for him. They hoped he liked them. He assured them he thought they were exquisite, beautiful works of art. And they were.

The table had been set for David. Some of the women had thoughtfully prepared some of their special foods for him in case he was hungry. They would leave him now so he could have some privacy. The leader of the group told David they would come back in the morning and show him his church, which was a few miles away in the center of their town.

After the people left, David looked around outside. Turning the corner at the back of the house he was startled by a rustling in a shrub. A six-foot diamondback rattler slithered off along the edge of the building. David quickly retraced his steps to make sure he had closed the door when he came out. He shuddered to think of waking up in the morning and finding a snake near his bed. Whoever carved out this new diocese was certainly no friend of David's. He was already hoping he could survive.

It was getting late; the sun was setting. David ate a little of what was on the table and took a drink of wine from one of the jugs. He then looked in every corner of the house and under every piece of furniture to make sure he was sleeping alone that night. He hoped he would not have nightmares. After praying and asking God for strength and humor, he went to bed. It took a while before he fell off to sleep.

In time, however, David adjusted to his new life. The people were appreciative of the slightest things he did for them. While there was little for him to do in comparison to what his other diocese demanded, he managed to contribute considerably to better the people's lot. With his contacts in industry, he was able to talk some of his friends into opening small plants out in the desert and developing little communities for his people. On a smaller scale he was able to provide training for the children so they could have hope for a better future. He started a clinic in the village and talked some doctor friends into taking turns coming out and spending time at the clinic each year.

Most of David's time, however, was spent doing precisely what the Pope had directed, working on his vision of the Church of the future. He didn't talk with the Pope as often but corresponded by mail more frequently, sharing ideas for change in the Church as they presented themselves. The Pope took a keen interest in what David was developing and continually encouraged him.

It was difficult for David to write during the hot summer months. The wind generator that provided electricity for his house did not always produce as much as needed during the summer, so David found it increasingly impossible to live in the house.

While touring the mountains one day he came upon a very nice log cabin in a high elevation where the view was beautiful and the air cool. He sought out the owner, who no longer had use for it. David bought it and spent much of the summer there working on his manuscript. The place was a godsend.

It was two years after David had been in his new diocese when he received the news of Archbishop O'Connell's death. He had not been in good health for a long time, though his death was not expected. David felt sorry for the old man. He wasn't really evil, just more in love with the Church than with the people. The big surprise came when Dick Franey called to tell David he had been appointed archbishop to succeed Archbishop O'Connell. David was thrilled for him. Still, he couldn't help but feel he himself was in a virtual prison on what was beginning to look like a life sentence with no chance for parole. Although he loved the people of his new flock, he sometimes felt as if he had been cast off by the Church to be conveniently forgotten, and it hurt.

The news which thrilled David even more came three months after Dick had been made archbishop. The Pope announced the appointment of some new cardinals. Among them was Cardinal-elect Archbishop Richard Franey. David sent his congratulations to him immediately, so happy for the man who had been willing to sacrifice his career to help David fulfill his dreams. It really could not have happened to a better person.

David's time in the desert was proving to be more like an extended retreat than an assignment as bishop to administer a diocese. There wasn't much to administer. His chancery consisted of three rooms. His chancellor was part-time. His secretary was more a receptionist who took calls and scheduled appointments for people who wanted to see him. David visited regularly the villages scattered throughout the desert. A four-wheel pickup truck was more practical for him than a car, because he had to cart so many things back home from his infrequent trips to the city, a two-hour drive away.

David's deep spirituality and natural toughness served him well. He could have spent the time there wallowing in self-pity, but that was not in his nature. In time he developed a real affection for the sincere, simple people of the desert. They in turn could see he liked them and enjoyed being with them. Although in his other diocese he never socialized or went to people's homes for dinner, in the desert he took turns visiting the families in their adobes and hogans. He became part of their families, and they came to look upon him as their spiritual father. His main desire was to inspire them to better the condition of their lives. The children were going to school more regularly, at first to please their "big father," then because they were beginning to enjoy it. David arranged for scholarships for children who wanted to go to college. When after two years students were being hired in the newly opened small factories, the other students started to show more interest. They seemed to have found hope for a better future.

Occasionally, David would leave his diocese for vacation or on business, but he spent most of his time there, being a good shepherd and working on his manuscript. In two years he was ready to send a draft of the manuscript to the Pope for his comments. Two months later a long letter arrived from the Vatican. The Pope was deeply touched by what David wrote and said he would like to work on the manuscript with him. He had some ideas particularly about the Church's central administration that would make it even more practical. Could David take time off to come to Rome and work on the document there?

After making arrangements for his chancellor to run the diocese and take care of things in his absence, David flew to Rome and spent a month collaborating with the Pope, listening to his suggestions and incorporating his ideas into the text. It was the first time the two men had seen each other in years, since David had been a semi-narian.

They were overjoyed to see each other. The Pope was impressed with David. He looked strong and healthy from his years in the desert, though the Pope had no real idea what the place was like and David didn't tell him. He contented himself with boasting about how deeply spiritual his new people were.

David was surprised to see how old the Pope had grown. The Pope had always been like a father to him; he had felt bad he had to be so hard on his protégé. David told him it was worth it, and reports from his old diocese proved him right. The diocese was flourishing. The people were growing spiritually and in great numbers as well. Even young people were finding inspiration from their faith and a home in their religion again. Both David and the Pope were pleased with what they had accomplished together, even though the price paid by David was so high.

David was even more glad his friend had asked him to come. It was as if the Pope had premonitions that his days on earth were numbered and he wanted to see David one last time before God took him home. He also wanted to make sure that David had a practical grasp of how the Church operated at the highest level, so his document would be not just a vision but a realistic and practical blueprint for the Church of the future. From his own experience the Pope knew how difficult it was to work one's way through cumbersome Vatican bureaucracy and bring about needed changes in the Church. David should be aware of those pitfalls in writing his book.

When the two men finished their work, David arranged for his flight home. The parting was painful for the two men. They both knew it would be the last time they would see each other.

David's trip home was filled with melancholy memories, of happy times as a young seminarian; of his parents, of whom he had seen so little during his busy life as a priest; of his many friends he loved so deeply and saw so rarely; of the strangeness of the life of a priest; of how totally dedicated he had to be to follow God. He reflected anew on how beautiful was his own call to celibacy, with the freedom it gave him to follow wherever God led him. He could never imagine his wife following him to the desert, nor would he have wanted a life like that for his children.

The plane landed in New York, and David spent the next three days on a side trip visiting some of his old friends before he went back to the desert. He was happy to see the progress made by Dick Franey in extending the programs they had started in the diocese. David was particularly interested in the little communities within each parish. Were they working effectively? Dick reassured him that they had been a stroke of genius. Every parish in the diocese now had optional small communities where people met on Sundays for flexible liturgies and the Eucharist. When they felt the need they could still go to the main church and worship with the large community. It worked well. People came to know one another and formed beautiful friendships. These tightly knit relationships became a source of strength and comfort in times of personal tragedy and hardship. Even the civic communities benefited, as people worked together on common causes

which brought new life to old and dying neighborhoods.

Dick told David he was able to ordain a large number
of older men throughout the diocese who were really like
the elders of old. They were given briefer training in
theology and scripture, and their only function was to
preside at the Eucharist for the small communities.
Many of these men were widowed. There were now well
over a thousand priests in the diocese. David was ecstatic when he heard that.

"How about the schools?" David asked. This had
been on his mind continually since he left.

"The schools have been doing much better than I
had anticipated," Dick replied. "When you dreamed that
one up, David, I never thought it would take off. However, I have been happily surprised. In fact, we have had
to put additions on a number of the schools because of
the increased enrollment. We have been so successful
we are now running into competition. We began to get
state aid last year, and ever since, some of the public
schools have been trying to interest industry in working
with their students."

Dick took David to two of the larger schools so David
could appreciate the enthusiasm of the faculty as well as
that of the students. The program was really a dream
come true. One important aspect of the enterprise was
that some of the companies involved decided to build
new factories in the area to take advantage of the well-
trained work force so readily available.

Dick took David out to dinner the two nights he was
there. They spent the time reminiscing about all the fun
they had had planning the radical changes that now

everyone took for granted. They were no longer considered radical but just the ordinary way of doing things.

David asked Dick how Ed Marcel was doing, and if the priests were still preaching Jesus. Ed had worked out very well, Dick assured him. That whole program had been a blessing to the diocese. Two of the larger Dutch Reformed Churches that were very close to Bishop Dorsey recently joined the flock. Their ministers had accepted assignments on the evangelizing team and were very well liked. The team itself had expanded its operation and had been in tremendous demand all over the country. Lately a number of women had joined the team. The women deacon program had also been well accepted, and a few more deaconesses had been added to their numbers.

David was glad he stopped off to see his friend. It gave his spirits a needed boost. Early on the third day of his visit, Dick drove him to the airport.

It was hardly two months since David's return when the shocking news hit the headlines across the world: POPE DIES. David heard from Dick Franey, who called telling him he had to go to Rome for the conclave and asked if David wanted to go with him for his friend's funeral. David wanted more than anything to attend the funeral but was unable because of circumstances in his diocese. Their conversation was brief; Dick was rushed.

The real reason David couldn't go was that he had no money. He couldn't put a burden on his people just to attend a funeral, even if it was his best friend, and even if it was the Pope. Had Dick known that he would have paid his way. David wished Dick good luck and hoped the next time he talked to him he would be addressing Dick as His Holiness. Dick merely laughed, though as a cardinal, there was always the chance, and for some, the hope.

A papal conclave is a grand affair. Cardinals come from all over the world to elect one of their own to succeed the deceased Pope. They are locked in the Sistine Chapel until they elect a new Pope. Carpenters and workmen of various trades work full-time readying the chapel with private apartments for each of the cardinals and two assistants. Kitchens are installed as well as sanitary facilities. Thrones, like choir stalls, are arranged along the walls, each with a canopy hanging over it. Each throne has a desk in front of it. In the center is placed a large table where the *scrutatores* count the ballots. In the back of the hall is placed a cast-iron stove with its chimney extending high up along the wall and protruding through a window. Overlooking the hall is Michelangelo's imposing masterpiece of the Last Judgment, with Christ presiding over the Judgment Day.

Cardinals were pouring into Rome from all parts of the world, reporting in and receiving detailed instructions as to procedure, what was expected of them, where they were to stay, who they were allowed to have with them as advisers, and other details they had to know.

When all was ready, the cardinals were allowed to enter and take their assigned rooms. Cardinal Franey was assigned to room 92. The cardinal on his left was from Japan, the one on his right from Canada. The cardinal in charge of the conclave, the Cardinal Secretary of State, inspected the Hall of the Conclave, making sure it was sealed off from the outside and that there were no interlopers present.

When all the cardinals had arrived and were properly situated, the doors of the conclave were locked, from the inside by the Cardinal Secretary of State, from the outside by a high-ranking member of the Vatican nobility. Everything was ready to begin.

The day before the cardinals had assisted at the Mass of the Holy Spirit, asking divine guidance for the important work they were about to undertake. Now they were ready to carry out their sacred task of electing a successor to Saint Peter.

All the cardinals were seated, waiting nervously for the balloting to begin. Printed on each ballot were the words "I choose as Sovereign Pontiff the Most Reverend Lord Cardinal . . ."

Voting for the first ballot began. One by one the cardinals rose from their thrones, walked to the table in the middle of the room, placed their ballots on the large silver paten, then tilted the paten so the ballot fell into a large silver cup. As each cardinal voted, he said out loud, "The Lord Jesus Christ, who shall be my judge, is witness that I choose the one whom I believe should be chosen before God."

Slowly the balloting continued. When finished, the vote counters counted the ballots, then read each one. The first ballot revealed thirty votes for Cardinal Giacomo Bianchini, twenty-eight votes for Cardinal Eugene Fournier, twenty-six votes for Cardinal Yashimoto Miki, twenty votes for Cardinal Mikhail Planikov, ten votes for Cardinal Jules Mobutu, and three votes for Cardinal

John Riordan. Two thirds of the votes were needed for election.

The ballots were burned in the iron stove together with straw to produce a black smoke that indicated no one had been elected. The huge crowd outside in Saint Peter's Square had been waiting excitedly. They were disappointed.

The second ballot began. Still no decision. The cardinals recessed for lunch. In the afternoon, the balloting continued. Three more ballots in the afternoon, and still no election. Names kept changing on the ballots, but none had the required majority. The crowd outside was getting impatient, and their voices could be faintly heard inside the hall. The cardinals retired for the evening.

The next morning the voting continued. Two ballots in the morning, another three in the afternoon, and still no election. The unrest of the crowd was increasing, as their impatience was rapidly turning to anger. People throughout the world, of every description, not just Catholics, were curious. World leaders were particularly anxious, wondering who would be next leader of the Church and what his policies would be on major issues facing the human race.

Back out in the desert, so many thousands of miles away, David had no way of knowing what was going on. He had no television; his radio he rarely listened to. His people were not fully aware of the significance of a papal conclave, even though their priests explained it to them in church, so no one brought David any information on what was transpiring on the other side of the world. He prayed at Mass each morning that the Holy Spirit would guide the cardinals in their choice. He prayed that, should God consider him worthy, his friend Dick Franey might be elected.

In the meantime, the balloting continued into the third day. Finally, Cardinal Franey, unable to refrain any longer from what was welling up in his heart, asked to speak.

"Brother Cardinals, my soul has been burdened for a long time now, and I feel I must share what I feel or my conscience will trouble me until the day I die. We have had ballot after ballot, to no avail. It seems obvious that none of us has been called by God. I would like to make a proposal. There is a man I have long respected as one of the saintliest priests I have ever known. He is also one of the most brilliant men in the Church today. He is an archbishop, and I was told by our late saintly Pope that he made this man a cardinal *in petto,* secretly. In fact, the Holy Father, before he died, entrusted a letter to the Cardinal Secretary of State testifying to that fact, so this man is one of our own."

Dick went on describing in detail all he knew about David's personal life, his intellectual accomplishments, his deep spirituality, his love for the Church, and his unswerving loyalty in the face of difficult opposition. After singing David's praises for over twenty minutes, he ended by saying, "This cardinal's name is David Campbell. I respectfully propose his name for your serious prayerful consideration."

The Cardinal Secretary of State did produce the letter containing the late Pope's message verifying his naming of David Campbell as cardinal and expressing his profound admiration for David's brilliant mind, his deeply spiritual life, and his extraordinary work for the Church.

David's enemies in the Vatican, though powerful, were few. Some were dead, others gone. Most cardinals had never heard of him. After serious discussion for and against this stranger's consideration, and after questioning Cardinal Franey and a few others who knew David personally, some favorable and some unfavorable, the next ballot was cast. David received five votes short of election. The next ballot produced an almost unanimous vote. The master of ceremonies made the announcement: Cardinal Archbishop David Campbell had been elected Pope.

The applause of the cardinals was deafening. The ballots were burned, and this time white smoke drifted from the chimney. The roar of the crowd could be heard all over Rome, though no one had the slightest idea as to the identity of the new Pope.

Inside, the conclave too was in the dark. How do they contact this man? It was all so irregular. But Cardinal Franey provided the information they needed. The Cardinal Secretary of State called David on the phone. David was sound asleep. "Bishop Campbell, this is Cardinal Franzetta. I do not have the time to explain all the details to you right now, but by the grace of God, you have been elected Pope. Do you accept the election? I must have your answer. The cardinals are waiting in conclave for your response."

How do you answer a question like that when you are woken from a sound sleep?

"Your Eminence, I don't know what to say. I just woke up," was David's reply.

244 JOSEPH F. GIRZONE

"But, Cardinal Campbell, I must have your response," the cardinal insisted. "The whole conclave is waiting. The people of Rome are waiting patiently for the name of the new Pope. Please try to give us your answer."

"I will abide by the will of God," was David's answer.

"The will of God has been amply manifest in what has taken place the past three days. You have been elected almost unanimously. That should speak loudly and clearly about the will of God. Do you accept that as evidence of God's will?" the cardinal asked again.

"I accept."

"Do you accept also your election as Pope?" the cardinal added, to make sure there was no misunderstanding.

"I accept that also, and may the good Lord have pity on me," David replied.

"David, you must take the first plane here so we can go ahead with the ceremonies. Everything will wait until you arrive," the cardinal told him anxiously.

"But I have a problem," David responded.

"What is that?" the cardinal asked, confused.

"I have no money to pay the plane fare," David answered.

"No money?" the cardinal exclaimed in total disbelief.

"Yes, no money, and I have no credit card. I live in the desert and no one has money here. I'll have to go to a bank and borrow the money. The nearest bank is over fifty miles away. I hope they respect my credit. When they ask what it is for, how do I tell them I was just elected Pope and I have to go for my coronation?"

The cardinal laughed at David's sense of humor, but

David wasn't being funny. He promised the cardinal he would find the money somehow and would be in Rome as soon as possible, hopefully by the next day, given the long time differential.

"One more question, David," the cardinal said. "What name do you take?"

"Name?" David said, totally caught off guard.

After thinking for what seemed an interminably long time, David answered, "Christopher." The name was the hallmark of David's life of bearing Christ to a world that had lost Him.

After giving David instructions as to what he should do, and also giving him phone numbers in case of emergency, the cardinal wished him good luck, and the two men hung up. David got out of bed and took a shower. He couldn't believe that what had just happened really happened. It must have been a dream. It could have been a nightmare.

David arrived in Rome for his election. He was dressed in papal robes and given the Fisherman's Ring, the symbol of Peter's authority, and led to the papal throne, where each of the cardinals approached and paid him homage as the successor of Peter and the vicar of Christ.

A vast crowd was waiting in the square outside for the newly elected Pope to appear on the balcony of Saint Peter's Basilica. Two members of the smartly dressed Noble Guard walked through the huge doors leading to the balcony, carrying the large white damask cloth with the papal coat of arms. This they draped over the balcony, then retreated back into the darkness. Everyone was waiting. Immediately a figure in white appeared.

There was an eerie silence. No one recognized him. A cardinal dressed in purple appeared beside the figure in white and spoke through a microphone. "I announce to you a great joy. We have a Pope, the Most Reverend Lord Cardinal David Campbell, who has taken the name of Christopher."

There was dead silence. Campbell? Who is he? He is not even a cardinal. How did they elect him? Where is he from?

Suddenly the crowd seized on the symbolic name he had taken, breaking two thousand years of tradition. Christopher, the Christ-bearer—perhaps it was a promise to bring Christ back to our discouraged world.

The crowd broke out in thunderous applause, giving voice to what they felt in their hearts as new hope for a new era being ushered into a world that had been about to lose trust in a Church that seemed forever locked like a fossil in an age long gone. Perhaps the Holy Spirit was still with the Church as Jesus promised, to bring back to a hurting world long divorced from God the compassion of a caring Christ, the Good Shepherd.

David walked out on the balcony and waited patiently for the applause to subside. Looking down at the crowd, off in the corner, he noticed the figure of a man dressed in khaki pants and a brown pullover shirt. It was Joshua. David was shocked. How did he come to be there?

The noise stopped. David raised his arms in blessing and greeted the huge crowd in fluent Italian, which took up its applause once again: "Viva il Papa! Viva il Papa!" "Long live the Pope!"